January

MEN AND THEIR CAVES

A wise son makes a glad father,
but a foolish son is the grief of his mother.

—PROVERBS 10:1

*F*athers and mothers react differently to life's problems. When I have a problem, I prefer not to talk about it. I want to go into a cave and quietly think until I find a solution. Women usually want to talk about problems, and the discussion takes the weight off their shoulders.

When I was the director of a drug prevention center many years ago, I learned that fathers would often write off a son who was into drugs. The attitude was, *He's not doing drugs in this house. He's out of here if he doesn't get his act together.* The mothers, however, were more compassionate and brokenhearted over a son who was caught in the terrible web of drug addiction.

Christians, we shouldn't react like the typical male. Instead, we should take the road of compassion and let the heaviness that comes with it drive us to prayer.

SOUL SEARCH: When have I reacted to something with a lack of compassion?

**Father, may I always react to all things
in a way that's pleasing in your sight. Amen.**

Moving Toward Wisdom

*H*ave you ever done something stupid and then regretted it? If you had put the book of Proverbs into action, it may not have happened. If you have wisdom, you will never do anything stupid. Proverbs has wisdom on friendships, work, sex, marriage, greed, lust, pride, and a hundred other pain-invoking issues.

The book of Proverbs is filled with wonderful wisdom for daily living—wisdom that can save the obedient ear much pain. While open-air preaching, I have often saved myself from being hit by remembering that a soft answer turns away wrath, or by greeting people gently early in the morning. So in the following pages I have chosen a proverb for each day of the calendar year, and along with it share a few words of application.

God gave us an Instruction Book for life. The world thinks it knows better, but like a climbing toddler, it finds out the hard way that life gives bruises. Pain becomes the teacher. Today's news reveals the hurts and tragic deaths of a world that ignores the Bible.

This greatest-of-all, most-hated-and-most-loved Book has been esteemed by kings, queens, and presidents. Within this divine collection of sixty-six books are the power-packed, pain-saving proverbs—a collection of the wisdom of God telling us how to deal with the problems, pitfalls, and pleasures of life. May God give you His wisdom from above as you read.

WHAT MATTERS MORE THAN HAPPINESS

Treasures of wickedness profit nothing,
but righteousness delivers from death.

—PROVERBS 10:2

What is it that you think matters most to God? I believe it is righteousness. We tend to esteem happiness as our highest ideal, and we say that it's the right of every American to pursue it. But righteousness is what we should first pursue.

I'm sure a bag full of stolen money would make a thief happy. But whether something is right should always trump whether or not it makes us happy. Most of this sinful world has no real hunger for righteousness, but it will be the only thing that matters on the day of wrath. That's when people will see that the righteousness that delivers from death is only found in Jesus Christ. I pray they will see it before that day.

SOUL SEARCH: At what times in my life has happiness meant more to me than righteousness?

**Father, please help me to always put what
is right above my personal happiness. Amen.**

January 3

HOW TO GET A FAT SOUL

The Lord will not suffer the soul of the righteous to famish,
but he casts away the substance of the wicked.

—PROVERBS 10:3

It has been rightly said that you and I are a soul within a body. The world is only concerned with the wants of the body, so people neglect the wants of the soul. But Christians understand that it's the soul that leaves the body at death and passes into eternity.

It is because of this that He denies the appetites of the body (the flesh) and instead feeds the soul with the nutrients that are pleasing to God—integrity, humility, self-control, the fear of the Lord, wisdom, understanding, and discretion.

If you're a Christian, seek after these godly virtues, and be assured that God will not withhold them if you cry out for them. He will not allow the soul of the righteous to famish, so do what Scripture says: let your soul delight itself in fatness.

SOUL SEARCH: As a Christian, how have I neglected my soul? What can I do to feed godly virtues in my life?

∽

**Father, please give me an appetite that will result
in a fat soul. Amen.**

THE MOST PRECIOUS COMMODITY

He becomes poor that deals with a slack hand,
but the hand of the diligent makes rich.

—PROVERBS 10:4

God forbid that we would ever deal with a slack hand. Instead, we must take a firm grip on life, realize how precious it is, and use every moment as a man in a desert uses every drop of his life-giving water.

Time is our most precious substance, so use it with the utmost diligence. Today, use it to further what is eternal. Just how can you practically do that?

Discipline yourself to read and meditate on the Word daily. Set aside time each day to pray for the lost and other needs. Walk in the fear of the Lord, always having awareness of His presence and seeking His smile above all else. That means you will guard your thought life, and will always be on the lookout to share the gospel with a dying world, either by gospel tract or verbal witness.

SOUL SEARCH: When have I been guilty of wasting precious time in this life God has given me?

*Father, help me to spend my precious time wisely today.
Amen.*

TAKING ADVANTAGE
OF TODAY

He who gathers in summer is a wise son;
he who sleeps in harvest is a son who causes shame.

—PROVERBS 10:5

How we should take advantage of the freedom to enter the harvest fields and reach the lost!

Imagine if, in years to come, it became illegal to give someone a gospel tract or to preach in public places. It is then that we will look back to these days of freedom and say that we should have been wise and gathered in summer. How shameful if we close our eyes and take rest when sinners are sinking into hell.

The Bible says that those who win souls are wise (Proverbs 11:30). So let's be wise today, and seek and save those who are lost.

SOUL SEARCH: How can reaching the lost—obedience to the Great Commission—be a priority in my life?

*Father, please help me to take advantage of today
so I will have no regrets tomorrow. Amen.*

WHAT WE WEAR ON OUR HEADS

Blessings are upon the head of the just,
but violence covers the mouth of the wicked.
—PROVERBS 10:6

Just isn't a word commonly used in the world, but the Bible uses it regularly to describe the godly. The entire human race is made up of only two sets of people—the just and the unjust.

The just are those who have partaken of the grace of God in Christ. They have been justified, made as though they never sinned in the first place. Jesus said of the religious leaders of His time, "You are those who justify yourselves before men" (Luke 16:15). That's all religion can do. It can't justify us before God.

How incredible that in Christ we are righteous in the sight of our Creator—and that on the day of judgment, instead of coming under God's wrath for our sins, we can instead hear Him say, "Well done, good and faithful servant" (Matthew 25:21). Blessings are on the head of the just.

SOUL SEARCH: Considering how I have spent my life, in what ways would God be justified in saying, "Well done, good and faithful servant"?

⌒

Father, help me to fully understand the incredible blessing and reprieve of being justified by faith. Amen.

WHAT GOD HAS FORGOTTEN

The memory of the just is blessed,
but the name of the wicked shall rot.

—PROVERBS 10:7

*I*f we are in Christ, we are able to do something that God cannot do. We can remember our past sins. He has cast them into the sea of forgetfulness (see Micah 7:19), but it's good for us to regularly recall them—without any affection toward them or condemnation from them, of course.

Jesus said that he who is forgiven much, loves much (see Luke 7:47). It's the knowledge of what I have been forgiven that wells gratitude in my heart and makes me love God all the more for the cross. Do you know what you've been forgiven?

SOUL SEARCH: How can I remember God's great love for me today?

**Father, I shudder when I remember my past sins,
and I rejoice that you've forgotten them because
of your everlasting mercy. Amen.**

THE WISE MASTER BUILDER

The wise in heart will receive commandments,
but a prating fool will fall.
—PROVERBS 10:8

It's refreshing to witness to someone who has a humble heart. Humility is the light by which sinners see the cross. The wise in heart will receive commandments, and God commands all people everywhere to repent.

As Christians, we are tuned to the will of God. Our obedience is evidence of our love for the Lord. And we are wise to always look for His smile, because in our obedience we are building our house upon the rock. When the storms of life come, we will stand strong because of our unshakable foundation.

SOUL SEARCH: In my life, what times of disobedience have I left unconfessed? How can I strengthen my foundation through obedience to God's commands?

**Father, help me today to have a
joyfully obedient heart to seek your smile. Amen.**

January 9

HEADING NORTH

He that walks uprightly walks surely:
but he that perverts his ways shall be known.
—PROVERBS 10:9 AKJV

To walk uprightly means to seek righteousness, as a compass needle seeks out north. Today, sin will try to pull the needle down. It may come in the form of pride, lust, jealousy, envy, gossip, or a thousand other sins—from the love of the world, to the love of money, to idleness and greed.

Don't buckle. Don't pervert your way. Let love for God be your shield against the enemy. If you love God, you will seek to please Him above yourself. That's all you need for your walk to be sure.

SOUL SEARCH: What are some hidden sins that I have a secret affection for in my heart?

⁓

**Father, help me not compromise with sin today,
not even for a second. Amen.**

IN THE WINK OF AN EYE

He who winks with the eye causes trouble,
but a prating fool will fall.
—PROVERBS 10:10

A human wink can convey a subtle message. It can be a warm greeting to a friend or a passing greeting to a stranger, or it can be flirtatious. If done behind someone's back, it can be a sign that the winker is being malicious or lacking sincerity. David said, "Do not let those gloat over me who are my enemies without cause; do not let those who hate me without reason maliciously wink the eye" (Psalm 35:19 NIV).

Of all people, Christians must be sincere in all of their dealings. The hypocrite winks with his eye. He says one thing and means another. Avoid such actions as you would the plague. They will only cause sorrow.

SOUL SEARCH: How have I ever deliberately been insincere or had bad motives in my dealings with others?

∽

**Father, help me to be completely sincere,
especially when it comes to sharing the gospel. Amen.**

WORDS FROM THE WELL

The mouth of the righteous is a well of life,
but violence covers the mouth of the wicked.

—PROVERBS 10:11

*L*ife and death are certainly in the power of the tongue
(Proverbs 18:21). Negative words can bring us down,
and encouraging words can lift us up.

However, because we are made righteous in Christ, when
we use our mouths to share the gospel with the unsaved, we
speak more than words of encouragement. They are words of
life, drawn from the wells of salvation. So never tire of sharing
the gospel. Your words, when used by God, are like life-giving
water to a dying man.

SOUL SEARCH: When have I avoided sharing the gospel
with others because of my pride or my fear?

Father, give me the opportunity to overcome
my fears and share words of life today. Amen.

January 12

MOUNTAINS AND MOLEHILLS

Hatred stirs up strife,
but love covers all sins.

—PROVERBS 10:12

It's often a challenge when someone sins against us. We naturally want to talk about the person to invoke sympathy for ourselves. Yet love covers the sin. It overlooks it. It shows grace and mercy, and it does so in the light of Calvary's cross.

If God's love can overlook our mountain of sin, we can overlook the molehill of someone else's sin. Such godliness guards our hearts against gossip, and against the subtlety of bitterness.

SOUL SEARCH: What reoccurring memories do I have that evoke negative thoughts toward somebody?

⌒

**Father, may I never lose sight of
what I have been forgiven in Christ. Amen.**

THE POWER OF UNDERSTANDING

Wisdom is found on the lips of him who has understanding,
but a rod is for the back of him who is devoid of understanding.

—PROVERBS 10:13

nderstanding is the light by which we see the gospel. According to Jesus (in the parable of the sower), the true convert is he who "hears … and understands" (Matthew 13:23).

Philip saw fit to ask the Ethiopian eunuch, "Do you understand what you're reading?" (Acts 8:30). Without understanding, there can be no knowledge of sin, and the Law (the first five books of the Bible, known as the Pentateuch) is the schoolmaster that produces the knowledge of sin. The Bible says of the ungodly, "There is none who understands" (Romans 3:11). This is why we must use the rod of the Law on the backs of those who are void of understanding. This is what Jesus did with the rich young ruler (see Matthew 19:16-22), and it was the testimony of the apostle Paul (see Romans 7:13). The Law brought death to him and acted as a schoolmaster to bring him to Christ.

SOUL SEARCH: How have I proven that I truly understand the gravity of my sins and appreciate what I have been forgiven in Christ?

*Father, please teach me how to bring sinners
to the foot of the cross. Amen.*

WHAT SHOULD BE OUR PASSION?

Wise people store up knowledge,
but the mouth of the fool is near destruction.
—PROVERBS 10:14

The knowledge we lay up will be dependent upon our worldview. Do we see the church as a lifeboat surrounded by a drowning world? Then we have a biblical worldview.

All around us are dying sinners sinking into an icy grave, and we have been entrusted with the message that saves. How then can we let anything but the salvation of the lost be our passion? Little else should matter. The knowledge we lay up is the knowledge of how, with the help of God, we can reach them.

May God make us wise with evangelistic knowledge, for he that wins souls is wise.

SOUL SEARCH: In what ways do I show that I really care about the salvation of this world, and in what ways do I show that I care more about myself?

Father, let me be wise with my time today and use it in some way to bring sinners to Christ. Amen.

January 15

THE RICHES THAT MATTER

The rich man's wealth is his strong city;
the destruction of the poor is their poverty.

—PROVERBS 10:15

God forbid that we would build ourselves a strong city without a godly foundation. Strong and prosperous cities without God are dry straw waiting for His wrath.

The Scriptures warn that riches don't profit us in the day of wrath, but righteousness delivers from death (Proverbs 11:4). Riches may open doors in this life, but not in the next. It is far better to be poor and daily on our knees for the next meal than to feast sumptuously on plates of gold and end up damned.

SOUL SEARCH: If I were given $10 million, how much would I spend on myself?

∽

**Father, today may I strive be rich in the things
that matter to you. Amen.**

January 16

THE HIGHEST PROFESSION

The labor of the righteous leads to life,
the wages of the wicked to sin.

—PROVERBS 10:16

We tend to think of a laborer as having a menial profession, but those who labor in the gospel are skilled laborers, workers who need not be ashamed. One can detect a laborer with the shake of a hand. A laborer's hand has both muscle and callouses.

That's also what a lifestyle of evangelism will do for you. It will give you a strong grip on how to present the gospel to the hardest of hearts. Our labor is never in vain, because we labor in the harvest that leads to life.

SOUL SEARCH: How much of my time do I spend studying how to share the gospel?

Father, help me to be a worker who is never ashamed (2 Timothy 2:15). Amen.

THE OBEDIENT HEART

He who keeps instruction is in the way of life,
but he who refuses correction goes astray.

—PROVERBS 10:17

"There is a way that seems right to a man," but the end of that way is "the way of death" (Proverbs 14:12). That's the path we were going down when we, like sheep, were going astray. But now we have returned to the Good Shepherd and Bishop of our souls, who leads us in the path of righteousness.

While salvation is by grace alone, those who have tasted the grace of God will have an obedient heart. We keep instruction—living for the will of God—not to be saved, but because we are saved.

SOUL SEARCH: In what ways do I delight in doing the will of God?

**Father, help me to always have an obedient ear
for your voice. Amen.**

THE GREAT REVELATION

Whoever hides hatred has lying lips,
and whoever spreads slander is a fool.

—PROVERBS 10:18

It is great revelation for a Christian to understand that nothing is hidden. There's no such thing as a secret, or something that no one knows.

God knows everything. Nothing is hidden from His eyes. Such knowledge keeps us walking in the fear of the Lord, keeping our hearts free from hatred, lying, or slander.

Let's be wise today and fear the Lord—because He warns that He will bring every work into judgment. And let's always keep our hearts free from sin.

SOUL SEARCH: In what ways do I show that I have a biblical revelation of the character of God and truly fear Him?

∽

**Father, please teach me how to walk in the fear of you.
Amen.**

THE BRAIN-FREE TONGUE

In the multitude of words sin is not lacking,
but he who restrains his lips is wise.
—PROVERBS 10:19

If your words have ever gotten you into trouble, you're not alone. The Bible says that the tongue is "a world of iniquity" (James 3:6). Sometimes it seems to work independent of our brain and say things that turn out to be thoughtless.

The psalmist pleaded with God to set a watch (a guard) over his lips, because his brain wasn't enough. Perhaps the "watch" is the fear of the Lord. If we can soak our brains in the thought of God's smile or frown at our words, we will be wise—and save ourselves and others much pain.

SOUL SEARCH: When was the last time I used my lips unwisely? What did I learn from that?

Father, please set a guard before my lips today.
Amen.

SALTY TONGUE

The tongue of the righteous is choice silver;
the heart of the wicked is worth little.

—PROVERBS 10:20

*C*hoice silver has been refined in fire, and those with a tongue like choice silver are often those who have been through fiery trials. A broken spirit has produced in them a sanctified tongue, and their speech is seasoned with salt. They speak words of life because their sinful nature has been put to death on the cross.

May we be wise in our speech today, not only with our fellow Christians but also with those lost sinners who sit in the shadow of death. May our words be light to them.

SOUL SEARCH: In what ways do I have a broken spirit?

**Father, help my speech to always be tasteful,
seasoned with salt. Amen.**

THE MISSION FIELD TO MILLIONS

The lips of the righteous feed many,
but fools die for want of wisdom.

—PROVERBS 10:21

*N*ow, more than any other time in history, is this verse true. God has entrusted us with the gospel that gives access to the Bread of Life, and our lips can potentially feed millions. We can nourish many with our words, whether they are spoken or written.

When I became a Christian back in 1972, I immediately purchased a printing press and began writing and printing tracts, eventually distributing hundreds of millions of them. Yet I'm no one special. All I have is a love for God and for the lost. So what's stopping you from doing the same?

The Internet is your mission field. Use it to feed many.

SOUL SEARCH: How much of each day do I devote to reaching those who, without the Savior, will end up in hell?

Father, use me this day to reach those who are sitting in the shadow of death. Amen.

SORROWLESS RICHES

The blessing of the LORD makes one rich,
and He adds no sorrow with it.

—PROVERBS 10:22

*T*his verse is fodder for prosperity preachers, and there's simply no arguing with it: "The blessing of the LORD makes one rich." The problem with these preachers, however, isn't what they say; it's what they don't say. They don't talk about sin, righteousness, or judgment. They don't preach Christ crucified for the sin of the world, but of the riches of the professed believer.

And so these preachers teach that gain is godliness, and they are filled with covetous practices and have millions of followers who are strangers to genuine conversion.

SOUL SEARCH: How do I know that I have sound doctrine?

◌

**Father, please help me to be as concerned about
my neighbor's salvation as I am about my own. Amen.**

THE BIGGEST LOSERS

To do evil is like sport to a fool,
but a man of understanding has wisdom.
—PROVERBS 10:23

Sport gives billions of us great pleasure, whether it is Ping-Pong in China, rugby in New Zealand, soccer in Brazil, basketball in the United States, or skiing in the Swiss Alps. We love the competitive nature, the challenge, and the win.

Theft is sport to a fool. He gets a sense of challenge when he plans his crime, and a sense of joy when the spoil is in his sinful hands. What he doesn't understand is that what is sport to him is wickedness to a holy Creator, who warns that thieves will end up losers, damned in hell. The joy that sin delivers is eternally outweighed by its fearful wages.

SOUL SEARCH: How have I truly divorced myself from affection to sin?

*Father, help me never to be intrigued
by the pleasures of any sin. Amen.*

THE KING TO WHOM WE OWE NO ALLEGIANCE

*The fear of the wicked will come upon him,
and the desire of the righteous will be granted.*

—PROVERBS 10:24

I would surmise that death is the greatest fear of the wicked. And it shall certainly come upon them. The Bible says that sinners are all their lifetime tormented by the fear of it (Hebrews 2:14–15), calling it in the Old Testament "the king of terrors" (Job 18:14).

Our hearts should break at the thought of any human being dying without faith in Jesus. We should be horrified by thoughts of them being terrorized by fear as they pass from this life into what they see as the unknown. May such thoughts cause compassion to overcome our own fears, so we never hold back from sharing the gospel. May that be the desire of the righteous.

SOUL SEARCH: In what ways is my gratitude in proportion to my forgiveness in Christ?

**Father, words can't express my gratitude for how
you saved me from death. Amen.**

January 25

TORNADO IN THE FORECAST

When the whirlwind passes by, the wicked is no more,
but the righteous has an everlasting foundation.

—PROVERBS 10:25

Most of us, because of the advent of video, are familiar with the destruction of a whirlwind, nowadays called a tornado. Years ago, I visited a town in Oklahoma just after a killer tornado and stood in both awe and horror at its power. It took human life, picked up cars, destroyed houses, and even ripped the bark off trees.

On judgment day, every covering of sin will be ripped away and exposed before the eyes of a holy God. Thank the Lord for His infinite mercy and great kindness in taking us out of the path of the tornado and establishing our feet on the Rock of Ages.

SOUL SEARCH: How often do I meditate on what hell is going to be like for the ungodly?

~

**Father, please give me a love that will cast out fear
(1 John 4:18) and warn the wicked. Amen.**

LAZINESS VS. DILIGENCE

As vinegar to the teeth and smoke to the eyes,
so is the lazy man to those who send him.
—PROVERBS 10:26

"As vinegar to the teeth" is probably the biblical equivalent of having our "teeth set on edge." Certain things, such as fingernails being scraped on a chalkboard or a fork being pulled through closed teeth, are included in this category. No one thinks that these things (or the painful experience of having smoke in the eyes) are pleasant.

As well, it is painful to ask a lazy person to do a job. May none of us fall into the category of sluggard when it comes to the task God has entrusted us with.

SOUL SEARCH: On a report card, how would God grade me for diligence?

∽

**Father, make me diligent in all things that please you.
Amen.**

THE SAFETY
OF FEARING GOD

The fear of the LORD prolongs days,
but the years of the wicked will be shortened.
—PROVERBS 10:27

The ungodly live for whatever gives them pleasure. They therefore involve themselves in illegal activities and risk their lives with illegal drugs. They indulge in alcohol and even drink and drive. They are given to the love of money and ambition and to anger and contention. They habitually overeat and develop the associated killer diseases. They smoke cigarettes, speed in fast cars, go through red lights, and risk their lives in extreme sports for a rush of adrenaline. Their promiscuity brings sexually transmitted diseases, and they frequent bars and wild parties, where violence often breaks out.

However, the godly live God-fearing lives and are therefore protected from many of these activities that so often result in premature death. The fear of the Lord indeed prolongs days.

SOUL SEARCH: What unnecessary risks do I take? Do any of them put my life or the lives of others in danger?

Father, keep me safe in the arms of the fear of the Lord.
Amen.

January 28

HOLDING STEADY IN THE STORM

The hope of the righteous will be gladness,
but the expectation of the wicked will perish.

—PROVERBS 10:28

The hope we have in Christ isn't like the hope of this world. It is both sure and steadfast—an anchor of the soul. When storms send our soul into confusion and overturn our once-steady ship, we have an anchor that steadies us. Our hope is latched onto the promises of God, and His Word is sure. He will never fail us, disappoint us, or let us down, and the hope we have isn't just for this life.

The anchor also holds us steady in the face of the ultimate storm. Jesus said, "Be still," to death itself. What joy unspeakable we have through trust in Jesus, and what desperate hopelessness the world has without Him.

SOUL SEARCH: As I look to the future, what things do I still need to entrust to the Lord?

Father, may I forever be anchored in you. Amen.

WHEN HEAVEN STAYS SILENT

*The way of the Lord is strength for the upright,
but destruction will come to the workers of iniquity.*

—PROVERBS 10:29

*H*ave there ever been times when you've had to make a life-changing decision and asked God to show you the way to go? Just one word from Him would be all you need, because even if it's a hard road, you'll willingly take it because you only want His will. Yet God in His great wisdom allows you to use your own wisdom. Heaven stays silent.

Our consolation is that in Christ, we always have the way of the Lord; Jesus Christ is our strength. In Him our foundations stay strong in the storms that life so often sends our way.

SOUL SEARCH: Do I get secretly angry when heaven is seemingly silent about something that's important to me?

*Father, help me to trust you no matter
what comes my way today. Amen.*

THE SURE INHERITANCE

The righteous will never be removed,
but the wicked will not inhabit the earth.

—PROVERBS 10:30

As Christians, we stand in the perfect righteousness of Jesus Christ, and because of that, we will never be removed. We will inherit this earth. At the moment, it's still under the Genesis curse, with much of it being uninhabitable, covered either in freezing ice and snow or blazing desert. At the same time, it's wracked with tornados, floods, earthquakes, hurricanes, tsunamis, and the curse of weeds.

But the earth that the meek will inherit is free from the curse, and when we inhabit it, we will be free from disease, pain, suffering, and death. We will enjoy life forevermore. What a wonderful future we have in Christ!

SOUL SEARCH: Do I have joy now because I believe God has wonderful things in store for me? How does this joy manifest itself?

**Father, help me to always be eternity minded
and full of trust in you. Amen.**

THE WISEST THING
WE CAN SAY

The mouth of the righteous brings forth wisdom,
but the perverse tongue will be cut out.

—PROVERBS 10:31

The dumbest of us speak the wisest of words when we tell a dying world that they can live forever in Christ.

Does our mouth bring forth such wisdom? Have we filled our heart with biblical truths on how sinners can be saved, so the Bible's abundance comes out of our mouth? Can we say with the disciples, "We cannot but speak the things which we have seen and heard" (Acts 4:20)?

It's wise to tell sinners to repent and trust alone in Jesus. The proud may see the preaching of the cross as foolishness, but on the great and terrible day of wrath, they will be eternally remorseful for not having the wisdom to obey our words. May God help us to reach them before that day!

SOUL SEARCH: When have I been hesitant to use words like *repentance* because I'm afraid of the scorn of this world?

Father, please soak me in your wisdom today. Amen.

February

WE NEED NOT PRAY

The lips of the righteous know what is acceptable,
but the mouth of the wicked what is perverse.

—PROVERBS 10:32

It sounds almost heretical to say that there are certain things that we as Christians need not commit to prayer. But we don't need to pray about whether abortion, rape, adultery, fornication, and many other things are acceptable to God; the Word tells us that they're not. We also need not pray about whether or not we should help the sick or do a good deed for a neighbor. If we know what the Bible says about loving our neighbor, we need not pray, "Father, should I show kindness to my neighbor?"

Likewise, we don't need to pray about whether or not we should share the gospel with an unsaved person, because we have already been commanded to go into all the world and preach the gospel to every creature.

SOUL SEARCH: Do I feel a sense of guilt when I walk past someone who I suspect may not know God? What can I do to overcome my hesitancy to share Him with them?

**Father, please give me godly discernment
so I know what is acceptable. Amen.**

GAINING WEIGHT

Dishonest scales are abomination to the Lord,
but a just weight is His delight.

—PROVERBS 11:1

*H*ow easy it would be to glue a penny in an unseen position on the scales of your grocery store. It's the smallest of weights and would only add a few coins to your customer's totals, but each year that little weight would bring in thousands of extra dollars.

The reality is that this theft would be an abomination to God, and would take you to hell (see 1 Corinthians 6:9–20). The cost to you would end up infinitely greater than what it cost your customers.

No sin is trivial in the eyes of a holy God, so we should always make sure that we walk in the fear of God and the knowledge that He loves righteousness and hates iniquity.

SOUL SEARCH: Do I love what is right, and hate that which God considers to be evil? How do I show this in my daily life?

**Father, please help me to love righteousness
and hate iniquity (Psalm 45:7). Amen.**

BOASTING OF BRILLIANCE

When pride comes, then comes shame;
but with the humble is wisdom.

—PROVERBS 11:2

There's good pride—such as having pride in the achievements of your children, or national pride—but there's pride that's nauseating and poisonous.

There is something sickening about an Olympic winner who boasts of his brilliance. I would rather listen to a loser lose gracefully than a winner win poorly. Boastful pride takes the shine off a gold medal.

Pride also destroys marriages. When a little humility would pave the way for an apology that would bring reconciliation, some prefer to keep their pride and let go of their marriage and children.

God resists the proud (1 Peter 5:5; Proverbs 3:34), so we must resist the temptation to let it have its way.

SOUL SEARCH: In what achievements have I secretly put an overimportance on compliments from other people?

∽◦

Father, help me to see myself as I am. Amen.

BENDY FRAMES

The integrity of the upright will guide them,
but the perverseness of the unfaithful will destroy them.

—PROVERBS 11:3

I once purchased a pair of glasses that had a titanium frame. They were not only strong but could also bend and not break. The instructions that came with them said that the titanium would not only bend in every direction, but it would always "return to its integrity." That meant that it would always go back to how it should be.

In a world that would pressure us to be twisted, our Christian integrity makes us return to what is right. We look to the righteousness of God as our standard. We must guard our integrity not only for our walk in Christ, but also for the sake of our Christian witness. Nothing dissipates integrity like hypocrisy.

SOUL SEARCH: If I were offered a secret bribe of a million dollars, how difficult would it be to compromise my integrity?

Father, help me to always esteem integrity. Amen.

February 5

THE RICHES THAT PROFIT

> Riches do not profit in the day of wrath,
> but righteousness delivers from death.
>
> —PROVERBS 11:4

Wealth and status should mean nothing in a trial. Whether the defendant is a commoner, a celebrity, a king, or a president, the halls of justice should be a level playing field. This is why the US symbol of justice is a blindfolded woman holding scales in her hands.

If a judge is swayed by the riches of the defendant, then the judge is corrupt and should be brought to trial himself. How much less will God be swayed by the supposed status of those who stand before Him. On that day, there will be no bribery. The only thing that will deliver guilty sinners from the wrath of a holy Creator is the perfect righteousness of Jesus Christ, and that comes only through the mercy of God.

SOUL SEARCH: In what ways do I guide my daily affairs with one eye on the day of judgment?

Father, let me never forget the fact that you will "bring every work into judgment, including every secret thing" (Ecclesiastes 12:14). Amen.

PERFECT GRACE

The righteousness of the blameless will direct his way aright,
but the wicked will fall by his own wickedness.

—PROVERBS 11:5

Jesus said to "be perfect, as your Father in Heaven is perfect" (Matthew 5:48). Some commentators say that the
word *perfect* means to be mature. But God isn't mature. How
could He be? That would suggest that He was once immature.

Our commission is to warn everyone that we might "present
every man perfect in Christ Jesus" (Colossians 1:28). We have
to face a morally perfect Creator and a perfect law (see Psalm
19:7), but in Christ we are made perfect by the grace of God.

SOUL SEARCH: When was the last time I thought of this
world's sinfulness in the light of God's moral perfection?

⌒

**Father, help me this day to love the lost as much
as I love myself. Amen.**

NAUGHTY ADULTS

The righteousness of the upright shall deliver them:
but transgressors shall be taken in their own naughtiness.

—PROVERBS 11:6 AKJV

The Bible often speaks of "transgressors." They are those who have transgressed the moral law, and they shall be taken in their own naughtiness.

The word *naughty* tends to conjure up thoughts of a bratty child. But it means more than just a childish throwing of a tantrum. It carries a meaning of being wayward, rebellious, and disobedient. We were once rebels—children of wrath who were hopelessly ensnared by sin—but we have been delivered from its deadly power.

However, those who die as transgressors will be judged by the law (Romans 2:12; James 2:12). They will be taken in their own sin. What a fearful thing!

SOUL SEARCH: Going by my actions, are my plans for this day mine or God's?

~⊙~

**Father, help me to have an obedient heart
today and every day. Amen.**

February 8

BROKEN HEARTS

When a wicked man dies, his expectation will perish,
and the hope of unjust perishes.

—PROVERBS 11:7

Notice the word *when*. Our demise is just a matter of time. It may be years, months, weeks, hours, or even minutes away from any of us.

The expectation of the wicked is only for this life. He expects to be here tomorrow. He makes plans for next year. He builds a barn and says to his soul, "I have many goods laid up for many years." Jesus calls those who have no regard toward God or thoughts of their eternal salvation "fools." Their hope will perish because they are unjust. They are still in their sins.

How our hearts should break for the millions who are spiritually blind. May God give us the opportunity to take the gospel to them before they die in their sins.

SOUL SEARCH: Do I fully appreciate that I was once blind, and do I desire to guide those who cannot see? How do my actions prove this?

Father, please give me a tender heart that weeps over the lost and then reaches out to them. Amen.

RED SEAS AND LIONS' DENS

The righteous is delivered from trouble,
and it comes to the wicked instead.

—PROVERBS 11:8

*N*otice that the righteous are delivered "out" of trouble. We are continually in and out of trouble. We enter the kingdom of God through *much* tribulation. We live a life filled with Red Seas, lions' dens, and Pharaohs—"who did not know Joseph" (Exodus 1:8), with Potiphar's wife waiting around every corner.

Trials are sent to establish, strengthen, and settle the godly. The heat of the sun sends our roots deep into God's Word, and the pounding of the storms settle our foundation in Christ. What's more, we rejoice in tribulation, knowing that "all things work together for good, to those who love God, to those who are called according to His purpose" (Romans 8:28).

SOUL SEARCH: Keeping in mind that God is working all things together for my good, what things do I still need to give thanks for?

*Father, help me to trust you when
I face life's "lions." Amen.*

THE KNOWLEDGE THAT PRODUCES UNDERSTANDING

The hypocrite with his mouth destroys his neighbor,
but through knowledge the righteous will be delivered.

—PROVERBS 11:9

It is knowledge that delivers the righteous. It is the law that brings the knowledge of sin (Romans 3:19, 20; 7:7), and if we didn't "know" we were sinners, we wouldn't have seen our need of the Savior. God even said that His people were destroyed through a lack of knowledge of God's law (Hosea 4:6).

As we preach the gospel to a dying world, our aim should be to impart the knowledge of God in a way that can be understood by the lost. May God help us to do that, because Jesus said that the good-soil hearer is he "who hears … and understands" (Matthew 13:23), and it's knowledge that produces understanding.

SOUL SEARCH: Do I see witnessing as an argument to win, or am I trying to give sinners understanding that will show them their danger?

∕○

**Father, please give me wisdom so I am useful to you.
Amen.**

NEW WORLD COMING!

When it goes well with the righteous, the city rejoices;
and when the wicked perish, there is jubilation.

—PROVERBS 11:10

*T*hose who are made righteous by the grace of God yearn for righteousness. We await a new heaven and a new earth, wherein dwell righteousness.

How the city of God will rejoice in that day—when babies aren't slaughtered in the womb, children aren't molested, wives aren't beaten, God's name is not blasphemed, and teenagers aren't bullied. There will be no more racial prejudice, rape, murder, lying, theft, fornication, adultery, homosexuality, pornography, or violence. What a day of rejoicing that will be! May God hasten that glorious day.

SOUL SEARCH: Which unsaved people in my life does God want me praying for, and preparing to speak to them?

**Father, may I always keep the coming kingdom
in the forefront of my mind. Amen.**

SILENT BETRAYAL

By the blessing of the upright the city is exalted,
but it is overthrown by the mouth of the wicked.

—PROVERBS 11:11

*T*here are many ways a Christian can be a blessing to his city. The first is to proclaim the gospel to those who are still in their sins and don't see their need of the Savior. We can do no greater disservice to any human being than to betray them by our silence.

As Christians, how could we watch our neighbor starve to death while we have an abundance of bread? How could we let people drown when we have the means of saving them from sure death? May compassion swallow our baseless fears, and may God help us to speak boldly, as we ought to speak.

SOUL SEARCH: Do I have neighbors whom I'm allowing to "starve to death"?

**Father, please give me your heart
for the lost. Amen.**

LET GOD HANDLE IT

He who is void of wisdom despises his neighbor,
but a man of understanding holds his peace.

—PROVERBS 11:12

*N*ever despise others. Instead, hold your peace and love them, pray for them, and do them good. Never render evil for evil. If you are lied to, stolen from, bullied, hated, lied about, or even threatened with violence, simply commit yourself to Him who judges righteously.

The Scriptures say, "'Vengeance is Mine, I will repay,' says the Lord" (Romans 12:19). The world thinks it knows better, and so they open their hearts to murderous hatred and destructive bitterness. They do this because they are void of wisdom.

SOUL SEARCH: Who on the earth would I hesitate to share the gospel with?

**Father, help me to trust you to take care
of my big and small battles. Amen.**

DID YOU HEAR THIS?

A talebearer reveals secrets,
but he who is of a faithful spirit conceals a matter.
—PROVERBS 11:13

*D*oes the mere mention of some foods cause you to salivate? Maybe it's the thought of a tender and juicy steak or a moist chocolate cake.

Gossip has a similar effect on the sinful heart. "Did you hear about Brother Smith? I heard that he's having marriage problems. I wouldn't be surprised if there's another woman involved." Such talk may be interesting to hear and pass along to others, but in doing so we are doing the work of the enemy. We are called to be faithful, and "a faithful spirit conceals a matter." Many a good reputation has been destroyed by wagging tongues.

SOUL SEARCH: How does the omnipresence of God influence what I listen to?

⁓

**Father, never let me be a vessel of gossip.
Amen.**

WHERE
THERE IS WISDOM

Where there is no counsel, the people fall;
but in the multitude of counselors there is safety.

—PROVERBS 11:14

*O*r most of us, seeking out counsel doesn't come naturally. This is because when we have our own plans, we don't want someone saying something to the contrary. It's understandable that we feel this way, because we see things from our own perspective. But others often see things we cannot. Many a time I've thought I knew best, until a humble and wise man said something like, "Did you think of…?" and I gasped.

Keep in mind that the Scriptures warn that all people do what is right in their own eyes. If you seek godly counsel from those who fear the Lord, you will find safety.

SOUL SEARCH: When have I wanted my own way so much that I didn't seek the counsel of others?

⌒

**Father, help me to draw on
the wisdom of others. Amen.**

WHEN WE
WERE STRANGERS

He who is surety for a stranger will suffer,
but one who hates being surety is secure.

—PROVERBS 11:15

*I*f you are going to financially guarantee someone, make sure you know them well and can vouch for their integrity. Nothing turns friends into enemies like a financial deal turning sour. If a stranger approaches you for surety and things go wrong, you are liable for his debts. Don't put yourself in that position.

Bible commentary writer Matthew Henry said that it was our Lord Jesus Christ who became a surety for us[*]—when we were strangers—and He certainly suffered for it when He was bruised and wounded for our sins.

SOUL SEARCH: At what times have I been irresponsible with my finances?

~

**Father, never let me forget the surety
of the cross. Amen.**

---

[*] *Matthew Henry's Commentary* (Proverbs 11:15), Christianity.com, http://www.christianity.com/bible/commentary.php?com=mhc&b=20&c=11.

THE GRACIOUS WOMAN

A gracious woman retains honor,
but ruthless men retain riches.
—PROVERBS 11:16

Grace and strength are not incompatible. It is honorable for a woman to be gracious. It is her strength.

In Scripture, the church is often likened to a gracious woman. We are to show grace (favor) to a sinful world because God in Christ showed us grace. He extended His gracious hand to us as we sat helpless and hopeless in the shadow of death.

And so we extend that same hand of grace to a dying world in the form of the gospel of grace. The harshness of a wrath-filled Law came by Moses, but grace and truth came by Jesus Christ. That precious gospel is the strength of the church. It's the power of God unto salvation, and in faithfully preaching it, we retain honor.

SOUL SEARCH: When have I let fear stop me from sharing the gospel of the grace of God?

Father, help me to always reflect your grace. Amen.

HAND IN HAND

The merciful man does good to his own soul,
but he who is cruel troubles his own flesh.

—PROVERBS 11:17

Grace and mercy go hand in hand. If you and I have grace toward others, very little will upset us. If we are wronged, grace and mercy will act as a bumper. In having those virtues, we protect ourselves from the self-destructive vices of bitterness, resentment, and hatred.

We have mercy toward others because we stand in the shadow of the cross. The everlasting mercy that came to us in Christ is never far from our minds. However, those who are wronged and lack mercy toward others become a poisoned vessel of bitterness. They disqualify themselves from the freedom that mercy brings.

SOUL SEARCH: What are some of the things that reveal that I have a short fuse?

**Father, may the virtues of your character
be evident in my life. Amen.**

February 19

THE SURE REWARD

The wicked man does deceptive work,
but he who sows righteousness will have a sure reward.
—PROVERBS 11:18

Those who serve sin do a deceptive work. They withdraw into the dark closet of their sins, deceived into thinking that God doesn't see their thoughts. Theirs is self-deception.

But those who love the Lord live in the light. They are without guile because they've been translated out of the kingdom of darkness into His marvelous light (Colossians 1:13). The godly no longer serve sin, but now sow righteousness in the field of the world. For them there will be a sure reward.

SOUL SEARCH: When God looks upon my heart, what types of deceit does He see?

~

**Father, thank you for your exceedingly great
and precious promises. Amen.**

THE ROBE
OF RIGHTEOUSNESS

As righteousness leads to life,
so he who pursues evil pursues it to his own death.

—PROVERBS 11:19

The world may protest the thought, but the truth is that every human being is a criminal, awaiting capital punishment, because we have violated God's law. Death will one day arrest us, drag us before the judgment bar of the Judge of the earth, and God's prison (a terrible place called hell) will be our just deserts. Without parole.

Yet the Judge is rich in mercy and offers a reprieve. He offers to forgive our transgressions, dismiss our case, and clothe us in the righteousness of Jesus Christ, and His righteousness leads to everlasting life—if we accept His Son as our Savior.

SOUL SEARCH: In what ways are my prayers sometimes selfish?

~o

**Father, I earnestly pray for the many human beings
who are still in their sins. Amen.**

THE BALANCED NATURE OF GOD

Those who are of a perverse heart are an abomination to the LORD,
but the blameless in their way are his delight.

—PROVERBS 11:20

It is good to read Scripture in its entirety so we get a grounded understanding of God's attitude toward the lost. He is not so oozing with love that He is incapable of other emotions that human beings exhibit. We are made in His image, so some of our traits (fallen though they may be) are reflective of His. God is love, but He is capable of justified wrath, and some people are an abomination to Him. He detests those who are filled with arrogance and pride.

Such knowledge is healthy for Christians. It means that we are careful not to have the contempt that familiarity can often bring. It also helps us walk in the fear of the Lord, which the Bible says is "the beginning of wisdom" (Proverbs 9:10).

SOUL SEARCH: What character of God do I have difficulty with? Or do I, without qualification, fear Him?

**Father, may I walk in the fear of the Lord
and be wise today. Amen.**

HIS DAY IN COURT

Though they join forces, the wicked will not go unpunished;
but the posterity of the righteous will be delivered.

—PROVERBS 11:21

Though the world joins forces in a unity of spirit and says that there could never be a day of judgment, let alone a literal place called hell, God will have His day in court. To maintain otherwise and believe that God will overlook evil is to violate the first and the second of the Ten Commandments. It's to make up in our minds a false god with whom we feel comfortable.

The sun will turn to ice before God will forget His passion for justice. Every murderer, rapist, thief, liar, adulterer, fornicator, blasphemer, and rebel who dies in his sins will stand before the judgment bar of a holy Creator and be judged by a perfect law. You have God's word on that, and there's nothing more sure.

SOUL SEARCH: Is God's Word my final authority on all things? How does my life prove this?

*Father, help me to show by my actions that
I completely believe your Word. Amen.*

February 23

PIGS' PRIORITIES

As a jewel of gold in a swine's snout, so is a fair woman
which is without discretion.
—PROVERBS 11:22 AKJV

I regularly frequent local colleges and universities to preach and witness one-on-one. I get to mingle with thousands of students, and I find it heartbreaking that almost every one of them has a filthy mouth. It's somehow worse to hear women cussing like a truck driver, because I expect more from the fairer sex.

A precious jewel should never be found in a pig's snout, covered with the filth that is normally on the sty's floor. As I listen to students use words that should make our hair curl, I can't help but think of the prophet's words: "I dwell in the midst of a people of unclean lips" (Isaiah 6:5).

May God have mercy on this people, send hot coals of revival, touch their lips, forgive their sins, and heal our land.

SOUL SEARCH: When was the last time I groaned in prayer for the unsaved of this nation?

~෧

**Father, please extend your mercy to this
dying generation. Amen.**

February 24

GODLY DESIRES

The desire of the righteous is only good,
but the expectation of the wicked is wrath.

—PROVERBS 11:23

"*D*elight yourself also in the LORD, and He shall give you the desires of your heart" (Psalm 37:4) is a favorite Bible verse of many people.

So what are our heart's desires? Mine are no longer for more money, a better car, a bigger house, and thicker carpet. I let all those desires go when I had my Gethsemane experience, when I said, "Not my will, but Yours, be done" (Luke 22:42).

Now my desires are no longer for myself. They are "only good." They have been aligned with God's desires—with a love for righteousness, justice, and truth, and of course a deep desire that none perish.

SOUL SEARCH: When did I have my own personal Gethsemane experience?

**Father, let your perfect will be
my perfect will. Amen.**

TOSS IT ON THE FREEWAY

There is one who scatters, yet increases more;
and there is one who withholds more than is right,
but it leads to poverty.

—PROVERBS 11:24

*M*ost things that are scattered don't increase. Try it with money sometime. Scatter it on the freeway and see what happens. It will disappear. However, there is a difference when the godly "scatter" their money—when they give it to the kingdom of God. It miraculously takes on the property of "seed."

When good seed is scattered on good soil and it gets plenty of water, it grows and increases greatly. So be careful where your scatter the seed of your finances. Sow into good soil—ministries that fear God and whose agenda is the salvation of the lost. Thankfully, there are plenty like that.

SOUL SEARCH: When was a time when I gave grudgingly?

**Father, help me to be a cheerful giver of what
you've entrusted me with. Amen.**

A LOOSE HAND

The liberal soul shall be made fat:
and he that waters shall be watered himself.

—PROVERBS 11:25 AKJV

*B*eing overly fat isn't something that many people desire. It slows us down, tires the body, and brings with it serious health problems. But the opposite is the case in the spiritual realm. Fatness of the soul is to be desired. The Bible speaks of the soul delighting itself in fatness.

A liberal soul holds his money with a loose hand. He is generous with compliments, encouragement, servanthood, kindness, gifts, and love. He also doesn't hold back from taking the gospel to the lost because of his pride. He takes care of others, and God takes care of him.

SOUL SEARCH: What adjective best describes me: kind, generous, loving, thoughtful, giving, selfish, or tight?

**Father, may I always be mindful of
the needs of others. Amen.**

MAKING MONEY

The people will curse him who withholds grain,
but blessing will be on the head of him who sells it.

—PROVERBS 11:26

The Bible is for private enterprise. God's blessing can be upon the head of him who sells. It's good to start a business and to make money. This is because money is the oil that makes the machine of commerce work, and without it we grind to a halt, both as individuals and as nations.

It is the love of money that the Bible condemns, or what we would more commonly call "greed." But money itself is incapable of evil, and so it can be used for good or for evil.

It's good to make money to take care of our families and friends, and to help others who are in need.

SOUL SEARCH: Who do I know who is in need today, and how can I be a blessing?

**Father, above all things, I want the blessing
of your smile. Amen.**

LET IT SHINE

He who earnestly seeks good finds favor,
but trouble will come to him who seeks evil.

—PROVERBS 11:27

*E*ven evildoers are capable of commending good when they see it. That's why we are encouraged, as Christians, to remember to be rich in good works. Good works that issue out of faith in Jesus obtain favor from God and from others.

The world may not believe what we believe, but they like what they see when they watch good being done. So feed the poor, clothe the naked, heal the sick, paint that widow's house, and diligently seek to express your faith in a way that can often speak louder than words. As Jesus said, "Let your light so shine among men, that they may see your good works and glorify your Father in heaven" (Matthew 5:16).

SOUL SEARCH: How could my light shine brighter if I took it more into this dark world?

Father, please make it possible for me to express my faith by my works. Amen.

March

March 1
THE SUPPLIER OF NEEDS

He who trusts in his riches will fall,
but the righteous will flourish like foliage.

—PROVERBS 11:28

It's money that provides clothes for our kids, puts food on the table, and pays off the mortgage, so the more we have in the bank, the more peace of mind we will have. Having money means it's less likely that we won't have cold, hungry kids who have no home. It's normal, natural, and understandable to feel this way.

However, it becomes sin when we forget that it's God who supplies our needs. He is the One who makes sure we can feed, clothe, and house our kids. So we must be careful to make sure our trust is in Him and not in our savings.

SOUL SEARCH: What do I still need to yield to God's ownership?

Father, today I yield my all to you, and acknowledge
that you alone supply all my needs. Amen.

HOW TO BRING YOUR HOUSE TO RUIN

He who troubles his own house will inherit the wind,
and the fool will be servant to the wise of heart.

—PROVERBS 11:29

The man who troubles his own house gets nothing out of it but trouble. He drinks alcohol and troubles his house by beating his wife, spending needed finances on booze, drinking and driving, and abusing his kids and scarring them for life.

He troubles his own house when he gives himself to the love of money, and greed steals his time with his family. He troubles his own house when he doesn't discipline his kids and leaves them without moral guidelines, reaping unwanted children, abortion, guilt, drug abuse, STDs, and bad marriages.

All these troubles come because the godless don't fear the Lord. May we never bring such trouble to those we most love.

SOUL SEARCH: When have I relied on my own wisdom to try to solve problems?

**Father, I need your wisdom daily to do what
is best for myself and those I love. Amen.**

THE LOVING THING

The fruit of the righteous is a tree of life,
and he who wins souls is wise.

—PROVERBS 11:30

*H*ow thankful I am that, by the grace of God, I knew from the moment I was saved, way back in 1972, that it was wise to give my life to the saving of souls because it was the right thing to do.

It's wise to seek the lost because it's the loving thing to do. It's wise to share the gospel with those who are on their way to hell, because God has told us to do so.

I thank God I didn't give myself to making money. Those poor millionaires who do so are rich only in the things of this world, and for this world I have neither affection nor allegiance. I hope you feel the same.

SOUL SEARCH: Is my outlook for the temporary, or am I eternally minded?

⌒

**Father, please make my life count for eternity
by making me eternally minded. Amen.**

DOUBLE MOTIVE

If the righteous will be recompensed on the earth,
how much more the ungodly and the sinner.

—PROVERBS 11:31

*I*f God sees fit to reward good, how much more will He see fit to punish evil. He will render to all according to their deeds. To those who trust in His mercy, He will give eternal life. So says the God who cannot lie.

If ever we should pause and meditate on anything, it should be on that: everlasting life! So we have a double motive to share the gospel. We not only want sinners to enjoy the pleasures of heaven, but we also want them to avoid the agony of hell.

May we use every spare moment of our precious time to work toward that goal.

SOUL SEARCH: What in life is most precious to me?

**Father, help me to number my days that I might apply
my heart to wisdom (Psalm 90:12). Amen.**

KNOW-IT-ALLS

Whoever loves instruction loves knowledge,
but he who hates correction is stupid.

—PROVERBS 12:1

*Y*ou probably know that know-it-alls are proud people, and they usually know nothing when it comes to what's important.

What's important begins in the beginning, with the book of Genesis. Life's jigsaw puzzle comes together perfectly when the Bible is believed, so that instead of confusion, we see the big picture. We know the truth, and the truth makes us free (John 8:32).

This is because God's Word instructs us that not an atom is held together outside of God's incredible power. Without reference to Him, knowledge is meaningless; it is clouds without rain, for "of Him and to Him and through Him are all things" (Romans 11:36).

SOUL SEARCH: Do I believe every word of the Bible is God inspired? If yes, was there ever a time when I didn't believe that? If so, why?

Father, thank you that because I know the truth,
it has made me free from sin and death. Amen.

THE FAVOR OF GOD

A good man obtains favor from the LORD,
but a man of wicked intentions He will condemn.

—PROVERBS 12:2

Millions believe they can obtain the favor of God with their religious (good) deeds. They fast, pray, repent, do good works, lie on beds of nails, and sit on hard pews. But when the moral law makes its entrance, it condemns us as guilty criminals standing before the judgment bar of a holy God.

The Ten Commandments show us that anything we offer Him is an attempt at bribery, and God will not be bribed: "The sacrifice of the wicked is an abomination to the LORD" (Proverbs 15:8). The only way we can escape the just wrath of the law is through the mercy of the Judge. Through the gospel we obtain favor—not because we are good (morally perfect) but because God is good, and He makes us perfect in Christ.

SOUL SEARCH: What do I trust in for my eternal salvation? Is it God's grace alone?

Father, thank you for giving us the moral law,
so we can use it as a schoolmaster
to bring sinners to the cross. Amen.

THE PROSPEROUS WICKED

A man is not established by wickedness,
but the root of the righteous cannot be moved.

—PROVERBS 12:3

God deals in the eternal. He knows what lasts and what doesn't. The wicked do prosper, but only in this life. The day will come when the stone of God's wrath will fall upon all evil, and Jesus said that it will grind to powder (Matthew 21:44).

His justice will be thorough, right down to every idle word we speak. On that great and terrible day, the ultimate storm will unleash its fury, and we will see the difference between those who built upon sand and those who were wise and built upon the rock. The righteous cannot be moved.

SOUL SEARCH: When have I forgotten my past and looked condescendingly at this sinful world?

Father, help me to always have a godly attitude
toward the wicked. Amen.

THE HARLOT CHURCH

A virtuous woman is a crown to her husband:
but she that makes ashamed is as rottenness in his bones.
—PROVERBS 12:4 AKJV

God sought a bride for His Son, and made her (the church) virtuous through His blood. The day will come when the Bridegroom comes for His morally perfect virgin bride, and she will be the eternal crown of her Husband.

But there is also a harlot church, one that is filled with false converts—those who have named the name of Christ but haven't departed from iniquity. This church is in bed with the world, and because she loves this evil world, she's an enemy of God.

It is this church that will hear the fearful words, "I tell you I do not know you. … Depart from Me, all you workers of iniquity" (Luke 13:27). She is a shame to His name, and "is as rottenness in His bones."

SOUL SEARCH: When have I done something that could be seen by others as hypocritical?

෴

Father, give me the wisdom needed to warn those who deceive themselves by playing the hypocrite. Amen.

THE DAILY BATTLE

The thoughts of the righteous are right,
but the counsels of the wicked are deceitful.

—PROVERBS 12:5

How would you like to have your thought life broadcast on *live* television twenty-four hours a day for a month? What rating do you think the viewers would give it?

Most Christians wouldn't want that to happen because they battle sin daily. Godless thoughts hit our minds as fiery darts from the enemy. These come in the form of selfishness, deceit, greed, lustful thoughts, uncharitable attitudes, jealousy, and every other sin in the book.

Our consolation is that when these sinful thoughts hit our minds, we deflect them to the cross and put on the mind of Christ. It is there that our thoughts are always right.

SOUL SEARCH: How would I feel if I sat with my family in front of a screen that showed all of my thoughts for the past week?

Father, let the words of my mouth and the meditations of my heart always be acceptable in your sight. Amen.

THE DEADLY ENEMY

The words of the wicked are, "Lie in wait for blood,"
but the mouth of the upright will deliver them.

—PROVERBS 12:6

The Bible refers to the demonic forces of this world as "wicked." "Above all, taking the shield of faith with which you will be able to quench all the fiery darts of the wicked one" (Ephesians 6:16). There is an enemy who came to kill, to steal, and to destroy humanity, one who walks about as a roaring lion, seeking whom he may devour.

But the godly open their mouths to deliver them. We warn everyone. We preach the gospel of Jesus Christ, which has the power to save. And we are able to do this because Father God "has delivered us from the power of darkness and conveyed us into the kingdom of the Son of His love" (Colossians 1:13).

SOUL SEARCH: How long does it take me to present the gospel to a lost person? Could I do it in less than one minute? Am I training myself to reach the lost?

**Father, today may I be a good soldier
of Jesus Christ. Amen.**

THE PRINCIPLE THING

A man will be commended according to his wisdom,
but he who is of a perverse heart will be despised.

—PROVERBS 12:8

*W*isdom is "the principle thing" (Proverbs 4:7), and he who "gets wisdom loves his own soul" (19:8). When Solomon asked for wisdom, God gave it to him, and the Bible says that He will give it to us liberally if we ask for it (James 1:5).

Those who have wisdom think right, do right, pray right, and speak right, and in doing so they save themselves a lot of trouble. Don't take a step without wisdom guiding your way.

Every step on the path of this evil world is a potential landmine, and so we need to ponder the path of our feet. If you know the Lord, regularly stop and listen. Be still and consider what God would have you to do that day or in that situation. That's wisdom.

SOUL SEARCH: Do I believe that I desperately need wisdom or that I'm wise enough on my own?

*Father, I need your wisdom every minute
of every day. Amen.*

THE HUMBLE SERVANT

He that is despised,
and has a servant,
is better than he that honors himself,
and lacks bread.

—PROVERBS 12:9

*Y*ou and I have a humble servant—the Holy Spirit, who Jesus said is our Helper. He points us to Jesus, and helps us to pray when we don't know what to say. He comforts us when we are despised by this God-hating world. He also gives us the power to witness, and we do so because He has shed the love of God in our hearts (Romans 5:5).

This proud and sinful world is without the Bread of Life, and so, as humble servants, let's take it to them so that they can eat and find everlasting life.

SOUL SEARCH: How often is everything I do soaked in prayer? Do I "pray without ceasing" (1 Thessalonians 5:17)?

**Father, thank you for the Comforter,
who helps us in our daily weaknesses. Amen.**

DOG BRAIN

A righteous man regards the life of his beast:
but the tender mercies of the wicked are cruel.

—PROVERBS 12:10 AKJV

don't like to think of my dog as a "beast," but that's what he is. He's a beast, and beasts lack understanding when it comes to many things in this life. He doesn't have any understanding when it comes to justice, the importance of truth, the beauty of music, or a good beat that makes him want to tap his paw, and he doesn't appreciate the beauty of a rose or the glory of a sunset. All he cares about is eating, sleeping, and chasing cats.

That comes close to describing most men before they come to Christ. All they care about is eating, drinking, and chasing women. No wonder some women call men beasts.

SOUL SEARCH: How often do I appreciate the God-given blessings I have that lift me above the animal kingdom?

**Father, thank you for opening my understanding
to what is eternal. Amen.**

March 14

DIG OVER THE SOIL

He who tills his land will be satisfied with bread,
but he who follows frivolity is devoid of understanding.
—PROVERBS 12:11

Are you "tilling" the land by cultivating the soil around you? How satisfying it is to be able to lay your head on your pillow at night and know that you've been faithful to the Great Commission? Christians who do the will of God by caring for the lost are satisfied with bread. God prepares a table for them in the presence of their enemies.

Evangelism is simply sowing the seed of the Word of God in the hearts of the men and women of this world. Jesus spoke of this special satisfaction as He talked with the woman at the well (John 4:1–26). And when the disciples asked Him if He was hungry, He said, "I have food to eat of which you do not know" (v. 32).

SOUL SEARCH: Do I find the voice of conscience to be a wonderful blessing or an annoying curse?

∾

**Father, please stir my conscience to do what I know
I should do when it comes to reaching out to the unsaved.
Amen.**

March 15

THE UNIVERSALITY OF SIN

> The wicked covet the catch of evil men,
> but the root of the righteous yields fruit.
> —PROVERBS 12:12

When evil men have fought their way into high political places and carried out their evil agendas, we can get the impression that evil is only in the hearts of a few. But there are many who would love to weld great political power and enact laws to carry out evil, and the opportunity just never comes their way. They desire the power of the catch that can be cast over the masses to bring them into submission.

But the righteous have no such agenda. Their root is not planted in the soil of this evil world. It draws its precious life from heaven, and yields the fruit of God's holy character.

SOUL SEARCH: Would I consider my unregenerate heart to be desperately wicked (Jeremiah 17:9)? If not, what would I consider it?

～◦

Father, I pray for our leaders, that they would be congenial to the proclamation of the everlasting gospel. Amen.

THE BLESSED LAMP

The wicked is ensnared by the transgression of his lips,
but the righteous will come through trouble.

—PROVERBS 12:13

*H*ow blessed we are to have the Word of God to warn us of the dark pitfalls of this life. It's a lamp to our feet and a light to our path (Psalm 119:105).

The wicked walk in darkness and don't know what causes them to stumble. They have no idea that life and death are in the power of the tongue (Proverbs 18:21). They speak angry words of bitterness and hatred, and in doing so, they open themselves to the demonic world that ensnares the sinner. And they are pulled deeper into the pit of sin.

In contrast, if the righteous fall into sin, they know the Savior, and in confessing and forsaking their sin, they are delivered out of trouble.

SOUL SEARCH: How often do I confess my sins to God? In what areas do I no longer want to stumble?

Father, stir me to meditate on your precious Word every day and esteem it more than my necessary food. Amen.

March 17

THE FRUIT OF OUR MOUTH

> A man will be satisfied with good by the fruit
> of his mouth, and the recompense of a man's hands
> will be rendered to him.
>
> —PROVERBS 12:14

How do you feel about words that were spoken during the day, as you lay your head on your pillow and whisper, "Search me, O God, and know my heart: try me and know my thoughts: and see if there be any wicked way in me" (Psalm 139:23–24 AKJV)?

The fruit of our mouth will reveal if we are truly rooted and grounded in Him. A tree is known by its fruit (Matthew 7:19–20; Luke 6:44). If we have a good conscience before God, we will be satisfied.

SOUL SEARCH: When was the last time I asked God to search me and see if there was any wicked way in me? What is my conscience saying to me today?

**Father, like Paul, may I strive to always have
a good conscience before you. Amen.**

GODLY COUNSEL

The way of a fool is right in his own eyes,
but he who heeds counsel is wise.

—PROVERBS 12:15

When it comes to important decisions, Scripture tells us that it's wise to seek godly counsel. It's wise because the way we choose may seem right, but the reason it seems right is because we're fools.

So protect yourself from foolish decisions that are based on emotion or selfish wants (rather than on truth or common sense) by surrounding yourself with those who love you enough to tell you if they think you're wrong.

The last thing any of us need are those we often call "yes men"—those who are afraid of offending us or losing our friendship.

SOUL SEARCH: Have I surrounded myself with godly people who will tell me the truth despite the consequences? What are their names?

Father, please help me to have wisdom from above
that's always open to reason. Amen.

LID FLIPPING

A fool's wrath is known at once,
but a prudent man covers shame.
—PROVERBS 12:16

*F*ools flip their lid the moment the water boils. Their wrath is known "at once," and there are plenty of things to heat up the water. Pity those in close proximity to such a person; they are the ones who get burned.

But the godly cover shame. They keep the lid on and let out steam through prayer. This is what King David did when he was angry. He prayed, "Break their teeth in their mouth, O Lord" (Psalm 58:6). But when the opportunity came to express his wrath, he showed mercy on his enemy.

SOUL SEARCH: Who in my life easily stirs anger in me?

⁓

**Father, help me to strive to have "the patience of Job"
(James 5:11 KJV). Amen.**

A CHANGE OF THIRST

He who speaks truth declares righteousness,
but a false witness, deceit.

—PROVERBS 12:17

The result of the biblical presentation of the gospel should be that those who normally drink iniquity like water would suddenly thirst after righteousness. This is the function of the law. It puts salt on the tongue of sin-loving people. It gives them the necessary knowledge that without the perfect righteousness of God, they will perish.

One thread of continuity through the Bible is its demand for righteousness. God requires moral perfection (in thought, word, and deed), and that's what we have in Christ. Like the penitent prodigal in Luke 15, we receive a robe from the Father—the flawless righteousness of God in Christ.

SOUL SEARCH: How important is righteousness to me in everything I think and do?

Father, cause me to "thirst after righteousness" today (Matthew 5:6), and to have a distaste for sin. Amen.

THE ACID TONGUE

There is one who speaks like the piercings of a sword,
but the tongue of the wise promotes health.
—PROVERBS 12:18

God delivers us from a sharp and cutting tongue. Many a child has been scarred for life, or a friendship destroyed, because of the hurtful remarks of the unwise.

James tells us that the tongue is "a world of iniquity … set on fire by hell" (James 3:6). Acidic speech does nothing but bring pain, scarring, and destruction. Perhaps its proximity says something about how we should rule it. If sarcasm or cutting remarks seek to pass through our lips, we should bite our tongue before our words do the work of the devil.

SOUL SEARCH: How do I react when people say cruel and cutting words to me? Do I forgive them?

◠

**Father, let my lips be used to encourage
others this day. Amen.**

TWO KINGDOMS

The truthful lip will be established forever,
but a lying tongue is but for a moment.

—PROVERBS 12:19

There are two kingdoms in this world—the kingdom of darkness and the kingdom of light. Through the new birth we are translated from darkness into light, and when we speak the truth in Christ, we are preaching what is eternal.

But sin is temporal. It is anchored to this transient evil world. Its pleasures are fleeting and but for a moment. Moses chose to suffer affliction with the people of God rather than enjoy the pleasures of sin for a season. But truth has been established forever.

SOUL SEARCH: Can I remember the moment I was translated from the kingdom of darkness into the kingdom of light (Colossians 1:13)? How do I know that I'm saved?

⟿

Father, in your great kindness, remind me during this day that I "wrestle not against flesh and blood," but against subtle demonic forces (Ephesians 6:12 KJV). Amen.

DOUBLE DECEIT

Deceit is in the heart of those who devise evil,
but counselors of peace have joy.
—PROVERBS 12:20

*O*ur sinful nature loves the darkness and hates the light, and in the darkness of the imagination, it devises evil.

But sin has a double deceit. Those who are given to evil may deceive others, but they also deceive themselves in that they think that they will get away with sin unpunished. They are like a man who he believes he can fly. He jumps off the fiftieth floor of a building, and as he flies by the tenth floor, he yells, "See, I'm flying!"

SOUL SEARCH: When my thoughts wander into areas they shouldn't, what do I do about it?

⁓

**Father, please never let me deceive myself.
Amen.**

March 24

NOT A DROP
HAS BEEN LOST

No grave trouble will overtake the righteous,
but the wicked shall be filled with evil.

—PROVERBS 12:21

God, in His infinite goodness, cancels out evil for those who love and trust Him. He shuts the lions' mouths, opens Red Seas, and exalts the imprisoned Josephs.

But He will also bring good out of places where we don't yet see the good. Down through the ages, Christians have been slaughtered for their faith. But not a drop of their precious blood fell to the earth outside the permissive will of God, and the immutability of Romans 8:28—that "all things work together for good to those who love God, to those who are called according to His purpose." His promise stands true for each dear brother and sister who died for their faith in the past, and for those who live for Him today.

SOUL SEARCH: How am I fulfilling God's purpose?

⁓

Father, may I remember this day that all things are working together for my good because I love you and because you've called me to your purpose. Amen.

THE TRIVIALIZING OF SIN

> Lying lips are an abomination to the LORD,
> but those who deal truthfully are His delight.
> —PROVERBS 12:22

*M*y heart trembles for humanity when I think of their trivialization of the sin of lying. They cross their fingers behind their back and lie through their sinful teeth. They call lies fibs and white lies, and yet with each one they are storing up the fierce wrath of almighty God.

It's been often said that taking the easy path is what makes men and rivers crooked. But what a poisonous river it becomes! Lying lips destroy friendships and marriages, and those lips through which the lies pass are an abomination to the Lord.

May we never forget what is offensive to God, and may we always be mindful of the terrible end of those whose sinful lips are given to lies.

SOUL SEARCH: What sins do I tend to trivialize?

*Father, may your holiness be forever
before my eyes. Amen.*

STORE UP THE SEED

A prudent man conceals knowledge,
but the heart of fools proclaims foolishness.

—PROVERBS 12:23

The godly hide God's Word in their hearts. They do so with the seed of the Word, what Joseph did in times of plenty. They store it up. This is because the Bible, which is ignored by the ignorant and mocked by the foolish, is the living Word of God. It lives and abides forever, and because it is life, it ministers life, comfort, and strength, and is a light for our path in this dark and sinful world.

So soak your sanctified soul daily in God's precious Word. Treasure it, search its wonderful pages, and meditate on its exceedingly great promises.

SOUL SEARCH: How highly do I prioritize memorizing the Word of God? What verse(s) do I want to commit to memory?

**Father, make me a faithful laborer.
Help me to overcome my fears. Amen.**

March 27

RISING BUBBLES

The hand of the diligent will rule,
but the lazy man will be put to forced labor.
—PROVERBS 12:24

*L*eaders rise to leadership like bubbles rise to the ocean's surface. They become leaders because they diligently set their eye on a goal, setting aside every nonessential. But like the slow-moving sloth, the lazy don't lead. They don't have a bubble to cause them to rise, so they are led rather than lead.

Strive to be a leader in the kingdom of God. Be diligent to lead in prayer, in holiness, in reaching out to the lost, in love for others, and in being a humble servant of the King. It may not happen overnight, but you have God's promise that if you are diligent, you will rise to lead.

SOUL SEARCH: Am I a leader or a follower? Why?

*Father, make me diligent, faithful, kind,
and loving this day. Amen.*

THE BLACK CLOUDS

Heaviness in the heart of man makes it stoop:
but a good word makes it glad.
—PROVERBS 12:25 AKJV

The law makes us stoop under the weight of our many sins. And as we look closer at its perfect precepts, all that does is add more weight. It thunders and terrifies. It banishes gladness and replaces it with the black clouds of wrath.

This was the apostle Paul's experience under the weight of the Law (Romans 7:10). He thought it would lead him to life, but instead it put a noose around his neck and condemned him to death. But Jesus tells all of us, "Come to Me, all you who labor and are heavy laden, and I will give you rest" (Matthew 11:28). He is the light at the end of the darkest of tunnels, and He doesn't merely bring a good word to make us glad. He *is* the good Word.

SOUL SEARCH: When have I felt the weight of my own sin?

**Father, it will take all eternity for me to express
my gratitude for the cross. Amen.**

March 29

BEWARE OF SIN

The righteous should choose his friends carefully,
for the way of the wicked leads them astray.
—PROVERBS 12:26

Sin is seductive, and the way that the wicked take seduces them. Its alluring flames toy with the moth, and unless God blows out the flame through the new birth, we are destined for death and damnation.

Jesus said that if we serve sin, we are a slave to it (see Romans 6:16). Lust puts chains on sinners and drags them further into sin. Anger consumes them, and hatred blackens their souls. Greed devours them, jealousy eats at them, and selfishness blinds them.

But thank God for His amazing grace. It rescued us from the devourer (Malachi 3:11). It broke the chains of death and hell, and set the captives free (Isaiah 61:1).

SOUL SEARCH: What percentage of my thoughts could be considered selfish?

**Father, open my eyes to the subtleties of my
own sinful heart this day. Amen.**

THE ULTIMATE PRICE

The lazy man does not roast what he took in hunting,
but diligence is man's precious possession.
—PROVERBS 12:27

*F*amiliarity certainly breeds contempt. We tend to take life's five senses for granted until we lose one of them. If we get something for nothing, we tend to undervalue it. That's why, if we have worked diligently for a wage, we appreciate it according to the sweat of our brow. We value most what costs the most.

Our salvation cost the ultimate price. It required the precious blood of the Savior. May a familiarity that breeds contempt never come near the Christian when it comes to the cross. Eternal life may have been free, but it was never cheap.

SOUL SEARCH: In what ways do I take my five senses for granted?

**Father, teach me the cost of my redemption.
Amen.**

THE WORLD'S THIRST

In the way of righteousness is life,
and in its pathway there is no death.

—PROVERBS 12:28

*I*f any word is foreign to this sinful world, it's the word *righteousness*. And yet our very lives are dependent on attaining such a state. Jesus said that if we thirst for righteousness, we are blessed (Matthew 5:6). But this world thirsts for the opposite; it drinks iniquity like water.

By the grace of God, we can see a change to that. The Lord has given us salt that we can place on the sinful tongue and see it thirst. The salt is the moral law. It condemns us and leaves us without any earthly hope of righteousness, causing us the look to the Savior to be saved.

That's why we must use that law as Jesus did when witnessing to sinners (see Mark 10:17).

SOUL SEARCH: How could I use the Ten Commandments to show others that they need the Savior?

Father, today let me put salt on the tongues of sinners. Amen.

April

April 1

THE FATHER'S INSTRUCTIONS

A wise son heeds his father's instruction,
but a scoffer does not listen to rebuke.

—PROVERBS 13:1

A wise son heeds his Father's instructions in Christ. He builds his house upon a rock, and when the storms of life come, he doesn't fall. He has God's word on that.

Being a Christian means to have an ear that is ready and eager to hear the voice of God. And we hear Him through His Word. If we are guided by the voice of our conscience, it will never go against the Bible. So let the Scriptures comfort you, guide you, feed you, encourage you, and even rebuke you. In doing so, you are heeding your Father's instructions.

SOUL SEARCH: What percentage of my decisions are made with the guidance of the Word of God? For what decision do I want God's instruction today?

⁓

**Father, may I be ever mindful of instruction
from the Scriptures. Amen.**

GUARDING THE GATE

A man shall eat well by the fruit of his mouth,
but the soul of the unfaithful feeds on violence.

—PROVERBS 13:2

*T*he mouth is the gateway to the body. If we don't set the guard of self-control at the gate, our appetite will take control and eventually bring ruin to the body. The eyes are the gateway to the soul. If lust, greed, jealousy, or envy take control, we will bring ruin to the soul.

Jesus said that we would be better to pluck out our precious eye than to let sin come in through that gate (Matthew 18:9). He warned that those who embrace sin will find that God Himself will cast their body and soul into hell. What a fearful thing! May such sobering thoughts help us to guard our sinful appetites.

SOUL SEARCH: In the last seven days, what have I said or done that was not Christlike?

✐

**Father, set an armed guard before my mouth, eyes,
and ears this day. Amen.**

GOSSIP OR GOSPEL

He who guards his mouth preserves his life,
but he who opens wide his lips shall have destruction.

—PROVERBS 13:3

*C*ontrol your mouth and you will control your life. Lose control and it may destroy you.

Our words can encourage or discourage, speak of gossip or the gospel, tell the truth or lies, or spread love or hate. The mouth not only makes or breaks human relationships, but it also plays a part in our relationship with God. Jesus said it reveals the abundance of the heart (Luke 6:45). With it we can deny the Lord or confess Him before others (Luke 12:8; Matthew 10:32). If we confess with our mouth that Jesus Christ is Lord, and believe in our heart that God raised Him from the dead, we shall be saved (Romans 10:9).

May our mouths be an instrument that speaks of the love of God so evidently manifest on Calvary's cross.

SOUL SEARCH: What past broken relationship have I never tried to repair? What steps could I take to mend that relationship?

**Father, may I strive to glorify you with
my thoughts today. Amen.**

April 4

THE EXISTENCE OF THE SOUL

The soul of a lazy man desires,
and has nothing;
but the soul of the diligent shall be made rich.

—PROVERBS 13:4

Those who say they don't believe in the existence of the soul don't know the definition of the word. The Bible uses the word *soul* and the word *life* synonymously.

When you were four years old, you didn't look like you do today. As you have grown physically, you've gained knowledge and experience, but you are the same soul. You have the same life within you, and that is what is motivating your eyes, ears, brain, hands, and mouth.

Lazy souls end up with nothing but unfulfilled desires. Use your life to diligently serve the Lord, and you will delight yourself in richness and enjoy pleasure forevermore.

SOUL SEARCH: What pleasure in this life tempts me most?

**Father, let zeal for your house eat me up
(Psalm 69:9). Amen.**

WHAT GRABS OUR AFFECTIONS?

A righteous man hates lying,
but a wicked man is loathsome and comes to shame.

—PROVERBS 13:5

There's only one who can rightly wear the title "righteous man." But, by the grace of God, all who repent and trust in Him are, in a moment of time, clothed with His righteousness.

The evidence of this is that we will love the things that God loves and hate the things that God hates. However, we shouldn't primarily hate lying because of what it does (destroys trust that binds relationships and usually leaves behind it a trail of destruction). Our hatred of it should rather be because lying is morally wrong. That's why it's offensive to God.

SOUL SEARCH: Do I really hate sin? How is this proven by my life?

Father, give me power this day to love the things you love and to hate the things you hate. Amen.

NO PARTY WITH THE WORLD

Righteousness guards him whose way is blameless,
but wickedness overthrows sinners.

—PROVERBS 13:6

We deny ourselves certain pleasures by living in the restrictive confines of righteousness. And so the world mocks us for our piety.

We don't party with them, and so we miss out on drug and alcohol addictions that destroy lives. We miss out on painful hangovers, drunk driving, sexually transmitted diseases, drunken brawls, wife beatings, and the guilt that comes with sin. We miss out on the broken relationships that come with adultery, and the ravages that come with jealousy, uncontrolled anger, envy, and bitterness.

As sinners give themselves to the pleasures that come with wickedness, they are overthrown by its devastating effects—and its final damnation. But the way of righteousness is blameless, thank God.

SOUL SEARCH: When making decisions, how often do I consider the devastating consequences of sin?

∽

Father, help me to see that it is for my good to deny myself the pleasures this world offers. Amen.

April 7

THE POOR RICH

There is one who makes himself rich, yet has nothing;
and one who makes himself poor, yet has great riches.

—PROVERBS 13:7

We tend to equate riches with wealth, whether it's large amounts of cash, stocks and bonds, gold, or property—and we can be tempted to envy the rich because they have it easier in this life.

But we shouldn't, because the odds are they won't in the next. This is because there are many impoverished rich people. They love their money and are desperately poor when it comes to loving God. Of all people, they should be pitied, because Jesus said that it is impossible for them to enter the kingdom of God (Matthew 19:24).

Fortunately, what's impossible for man is possible with God, and many a rich person has become poor in spirit, that they might be rich toward God.

SOUL SEARCH: When was a time when I envied the rich?

Father, help me never to put my trust in uncertain riches (1 Timothy 6:17). Amen.

PERILS OF RICHES

The ransom of a man's life is his riches,
but the poor does not hear rebuke.
—PROVERBS 13:8

I shudder when a couple wins hundreds of millions of dollars and has to make their so-called "good fortune" publicly known. Not only will they suddenly discover relatives they didn't know they had, but they will also become targets of criminal minds.

Such wealth instantly makes their precious children, grandchildren, and other relatives potential kidnap victims. I'm sure many a ransom has been quietly paid by the rich, in exchange for the life of a loved one.

Matthew Henry says of this verse, "Great riches often tempt to violence against those that possess them; but the poor are free from such perils."*

SOUL SEARCH: How content am I with my life?

Father, I pray for those who are so far removed from your kingdom because of their love of money. Amen.

---

* *Matthew Henry's Commentary* (Proverbs 13:8), Christianity.com, http://www.christianity.com/bible/commentary.php?com=mhc&b=20&c=13.

April 9

LIGHT AND LIFE

The light of the righteous rejoices,
but the lamp of the wicked will be put out.

—PROVERBS 13:9

Scripture often compares light with life. Jesus said, "I am the light of the world. He who follows Me shall not walk in darkness, but have the light of life" (John 8:12).

God, because of His great love, has translated us out of the kingdom of darkness and brought us into His glorious light. The darkness has gone, and the morning sunlight streams in through the window of our soul. It is because He has granted us everlasting life that we will rejoice with joy unspeakable.

But how our heart breaks at the thought of the ungodly being damned in the dark and hopelessness of hell. May His love in us reach out to them while we still have time.

SOUL SEARCH: How often do I rejoice because my name is written in heaven (Luke 10:20)?

Father, this day may the light and life of Jesus Christ shine through me. Amen.

WILLING BEDFELLOWS

By pride comes nothing but strife,
but with the well-advised is wisdom.

—PROVERBS 13:10

*P*ride rarely backs down from contention. It is head-strong, selfish, rude, arrogant, deaf, and blind. It is a monster that will verbally beat up our loved ones and then proclaim itself the winner.

Pride is the very root of our sinful nature, and it is a willing bedfellow with hidden conceit, an inflated ego, and worldly vanity. If we should hate anything in this life, it should be the devouring monster of pride. The Bible says that God hates pride (Proverbs 8:13).

The well-advised take their advice from the Master, and wash feet. They humbly serve their spouse, brethren, coworkers, the homeless, and strangers. If there is the slightest contention, they are more than willing to yield, and in so doing they conquer the monster of pride.

SOUL SEARCH: When is the last time my actions would have been considered headstrong?

Father, today may I have a humble servant attitude
before you and before the world. Amen.

GATHERING BY LABOR

Wealth gained by dishonesty be diminished,
but he who gathers by labor will increase.
—PROVERBS 13:11

It's not uncommon for professional sportsmen—from those in the NBA, to the NFL, to professional boxers—to quickly come into a large amount of wealth, and not too long afterward be in debt. It leaves most of us shaking our heads and wondering what happened.

The reason for this is that they didn't gather their riches by normal means. There was a sudden downpour of rain that flooded the land, and then it dissipated because there was not time for it to sink into the soil. But gathering by labor is a steady rain that has time to sink into the soil and bring great benefit to the land.

SOUL SEARCH: How much satisfaction do I get from labor?

**Father, help me to be diligent with what
you have entrusted to me. Amen.**

THE TREE OF LIFE

Hope deferred makes the heart sick,
but when the desire comes, it is a tree of life.
—PROVERBS 13:12

*D*uring the production of a documentary back in 1980, my cameraman captured footage of a violent gang fight. It was immediately seized by police to be used as court evidence. With permission from the police, we included the footage in the movie, but we had to wait for the trial to be over before we could release the movie. Every time I had a release date, the trial date was deferred and my hopes were dashed. Bills mounted up and I was put in a difficult financial position. My heart was sick.

The case finally went to court and we were legally able to release the film, and 2,300 people showed up to the premiere. That which made my heart sick became a tree of life.

We have a hope that is never deferred. It is both sure and steadfast. We are awaiting the sound of the trumpet, and when that desire comes, we will most certainly have the tree of life.

SOUL SEARCH: How much do I appreciate the hope in Christ set before me?

**Father, never let me lose sight of the glorious
hope that awaits me. Amen.**

MOST LOVED AND MOST HATED

He who despises the word will be destroyed,
but he who fears the commandment will be rewarded.

—PROVERBS 13:13

The Bible is the world's most loved and most hated book. The Word of God is despised because it contains the moral law, and it warns that God will punish those who transgress it. Romans 8:7 says, "The carnal mind is enmity against God; for it is not subject to the law of God, nor indeed can be." In other words, the sinful human mind is offended at the thought of God's moral government.

Sin-loving sinners don't want God telling them what to do morally, and if they stay in that state of rebellion, they will tragically end up in a terrible place called hell. But those who fear God will listen to the moral law when it accuses them of sin, and those who confess and forsake their sins will find mercy in Jesus Christ.

SOUL SEARCH: How often do I rejoice over God's Word, as one who finds great treasure?

Father, may I fully appreciate access to the Bible.
Amen.

April 14

ETERNAL PRIORITY

The law of the wise is a fountain of life,
to turn one away from the snares of death.
—PROVERBS 13:14

Whenever hell-bound sinners obey the sayings of Jesus, wisdom finds a place in their souls. Jesus said they're like a wise man who built his house on a rock (Matthew 7:24). This happens because God, in His great mercy, has opened the eyes of their understanding so they can see the invisible. Suddenly, eternity has priority over the temporary. They understand the light of the glorious gospel—that the love of God has made a way for them to depart from the snares of death.

They can now say with the apostle Paul, "The law of the Spirit of life in Christ Jesus has made me free from the law of sin and death" (Acts 8:2).

SOUL SEARCH: How does my life prove that I am living as someone who has found everlasting life?

◦⊘◦

**Father, no words can express my gratitude
to you for the fountain of life. Amen.**

THE TASKMASTER

Good understanding gains favor,
but the way of the unfaithful is hard.

—PROVERBS 13:15

*S*in is a cruel taskmaster. It keeps its slaves in chains, has a whip for their backs, and deals out the most undesirable of wages. The wages of sin is death (Romans 6:23). Like a drug pusher, it holds the opiate of sin in front of its addicted client, who becomes like a helpless and struggling fish on a hook. The way of the transgressor is hard until the One who has the keys to death and hell sets the captive free.

May you and I never forget the grace that unlocked our chains of death, and that our divine commission is to take that key to other enslaved and hell-bound sinners.

SOUL SEARCH: How guilty do I feel if I go for days without telling anyone how they can find everlasting life?

⤳

Father, please give me a conscience that will accuse me when I lack love. Amen.

April 16

WHEN MONEY IS MEANINGLESS

Every prudent man acts with knowledge,
but a fool lays open his folly.

—PROVERBS 13:16

*K*nowledge has the power to change our minds in seconds. If I offered you $10 million or a parachute, which would you choose? If you're normal, you would choose the $10 million, because you can buy twenty thousand parachutes for that amount of money.

But here's some knowledge that should change your mind. What if you'd been on the one-hundredth story of the burning World Trade Center on September 11, 2001? Now all that money would be meaningless, and that parachute would be everything because it could save your life.

The prudent man knows that sin offers great pleasure. However, he has knowledge that without Jesus Christ he will lose his precious life, and so he deals with knowledge wisely.

SOUL SEARCH: From one to ten, how would I rate my knowledge of the Scriptures?

⌒⌒

**Father, help me to be a reservoir of the
knowledge of God. Amen.**

AMBASSADORS FOR CHRIST

A wicked messenger falls into trouble,
but a faithful ambassador brings health.

—PROVERBS 13:17

We are called to be faithful ambassadors for Christ in a hostile and godless world. We are the representatives of a heavenly country in which dwells righteousness.

To be faithful to the message is not only to be faithful to God, but also to dying humanity. While the world would have us compromise on issues like sin, the holiness of God, and the exclusivity of Christ, we will not—because to do so would be to their eternal detriment. Those wolves in sheep's clothing who do compromise are wicked messengers who fall into the worst of mischief.

May we, in contrast, live to hear the words "Well done, good and faithful servant" (Matthew 25:23).

SOUL SEARCH: Do I know the Scriptures well enough to recognize unsound doctrine? What unsound doctrines are most common in today's world?

Father, keep my doctrine sound. Amen.

THE TWO PLEADINGS

Poverty and shame will come to him who disdains correction,
but he who regards a rebuke will be honored.

—PROVERBS 13:18

*T*he message of the gospel is one of rebuke. We are to: "Preach the word! Be ready in season and out of season. Convince, rebuke, exhort, with all longsuffering and teaching" (2 Timothy 4:2). We go places we don't want to go to, to say something we don't want to say, to people who don't want to hear it.

We are to call people to repentance—people who think they haven't sinned—and it's an impossible task to achieve without the help of God. So we plead with God before we plead with men. We ask Him to soften their hearts and open their ears, because unless He does so, they will refuse instruction and perish.

SOUL SEARCH: Do I ever hesitate to mention the word *repentance* for fear of offense? If so, how can I overcome this?

ᵔᵕᵔ

**Father, may I seek your approval and not
that of the world. Amen.**

THE SNUGGLE

The desire accomplished is sweet to the soul,
but it is an abomination to fools to depart from evil.

—PROVERBS 13:19

Most of us would qualify as fools, because none of us desired to depart from evil until God opened our eyes to the true nature of sin. Who of us understood that it is evil to fail to love God with all of our heart, mind, soul, and strength? If that is the greatest commandment, then the greatest sin is failure to fulfill its command.

Instead, we sought to fulfill our own selfish desires and snuggled up to our image of God, believing that we were morally good and didn't need His mercy. We loved the darkness and would have stayed in its shadows had not God, in His great love, brought the light to us.

SOUL SEARCH: In what situations do I find selfishness in my heart?

Father, help me to imitate the Savior's love today.
Amen.

April 20

FLOCKING
WITH HIGH FLIERS

He who walks with wise men will be wise,
but the companion of fools will be destroyed.

—PROVERBS 13:20

*B*irds of a feather flock together, so surround yourself with high fliers who fear God, and what they believe will rub off on you.

"The fear of the LORD is the beginning of wisdom" (Proverbs 9:10). Only those who fear God are wise. They will always speak the truth in love. They won't hold back for concern of offending you. They will advise you in the light of eternity and God's smile or frown. They will have godly priorities, shun sin, and live in holiness.

Those who fear God will faithfully watch your back, and as soldiers of Christ in the midst of the ultimate war, they are the ones with whom you want to surround yourself.

SOUL SEARCH: Whom do I admire? Why?

**Father, help me to admire people
with godly virtues. Amen.**

HEEL SNAPPERS

Evil pursues sinners,
but to the righteous, good shall be repaid.
—PROVERBS 13:21

As long as we are in this world, evil will snap at our heels like Pharaoh's army snapped at the heels of the children of Israel as they chased them to the Red Sea.

The Pharaoh of this world came to kill, steal, and destroy, and he will not easily let go of his slaves. Like a roaring lion, he walks about "seeking whom he may devour" (1 Peter 5:8). Notice the word used is *may*. It's a word of permission. Satan has permission to devour all those who serve sin because they are his slaves.

The only way we can stop evil from pursuing us is to put the Red Sea between us and its grip, and that's what conversion does. When we are born again, we are removed from the kingdom of darkness. We no longer serve sin, and so evil has no legal right to pursue us, because we are no longer sinners. We have been made saints by the grace of God; we are in a different kingdom.

SOUL SEARCH: How often do I consider that I don't "wrestle against flesh and blood," but against demonic forces (Ephesians 6:12)?

᠑

**Father, please open my eyes to the
spiritual realm this day. Amen.**

OUR INHERITANCE

A good man leaves an inheritance to his children's children,
but the wealth of the sinner is stored up for the righteous.

—PROVERBS 13:22

In Christ, God left an inheritance to His children and His children's children. Have you read what you have been left in His will and testament? It's very clear.

Look at these wonderful promises to His heirs: "And give you an inheritance among all those who are sanctified" (Acts 20:32). "And if children, then heirs—heirs of God and joint-heirs with Christ" (Romans 8:17). "To an inheritance incorruptible and undefiled and that does not fade away, reserved in heaven for you" (1 Peter 1:4). "From the Lord you will receive the reward of the inheritance; for you serve the Lord Christ" (Colossians 3:24).

We are going to inherit the earth. It's all laid up for the just.

SOUL SEARCH: In what ways do I stand firmly on the promises of God each and every day?

⁓○

**Father, never let me doubt your integrity
to keep your word. Amen.**

April 23

THE PLOT OF LAND

Much food is in the fallow ground of the poor,
and for lack of justice there is waste.

—PROVERBS 13:23

The poor man has his small plot of land that he diligently plows and sows with his seed. He tends it daily, removing the weeds and watering the tender plants. He is diligent because he has no choice. This is his precious family's future food, and he takes care so that its yield will be maximized.

Be steadfast and unmovable to till that little piece of land God has given you. Keep diligently sowing the precious seed of the Word of God in the hearts of your unsaved loved ones, coworkers, and neighbors. Pull out the choking weeds of misunderstanding by "speaking the truth in love" (Ephesians 4:15). Water it with good works (James 2:14–26). Those who sow in tears shall reap in joy. God's word will not return void (Isaiah 55:11).

SOUL SEARCH: How could I be more "steadfast and immovable" (1 Corinthians 15:58) in my labor for the Lord?

~

**Father, help me to steadfastly sow words of life
into this dying world. Amen.**

April 24

THE RUIN OF THE MOTHER

He who spares his rod hates his son,
but he who loves him disciplines him promptly.

—PROVERBS 13:24

There are strong words for those who fail to correct a rebellious child. Scripture uses hyperbole, saying that, in essence, a father is showing that he doesn't love his son, because he doesn't care about his eventual well-being.

The world thinks it knows better than the Maker, and so it leaves the rebellious child to find his own way through life. This results in a rebellious adult. You will almost always trace the lying, raping, murderous, stealing, blasphemous, adulterous, fornicating, baby-killing adult back to neglected loving discipline as a child. "A child left to himself brings shame to his mother" (Proverbs 29:15), and a generation left to itself will be to the ruin of a nation.

SOUL SEARCH: Is there anything in me that looks at Scripture and thinks I know a better way?

~

**Father, help me to always trust you above
my own fallible heart. Amen.**

THE HUNGRY MONSTER

The righteous eats to the satisfying of his soul,
but the stomach of the wicked shall be in want.

—PROVERBS 13:25

The psalmist said, "I humbled myself with fasting" (Psalm 35:13). While most of us couldn't go for forty days without food, we can perhaps fast a meal or two each week.

If you can do that, you will find great benefits. One is that the hunger you experience will cause you to be grateful to God every time you eat food. You will abound with thanksgiving, and that appreciation will make every bite taste sweeter.

Another benefit is that you will learn to control the hungry monster within that, if not restrained, will cause you to dig your grave with your spoon. It is the stomach of the wicked that will "be in want," and regular fasting will make you able to tell your belly that it may want, but it's not always going to get.

SOUL SEARCH: How satisfied am I in Jesus? What area of my life do I want Jesus to satisfy?

<hr />

**Father, you are my Shepherd; "I shall not want"
(Psalm 23:1). Amen.**

WOMAN'S LIBERATION

The wise woman builds her house,
but the foolish pulls it down with her hands.

—PROVERBS 14:1

*E*very wise woman works diligently to make her life stable, and she can do so through the gospel. Jesus said that those who are wise build their house upon a rock, and the immovable rock that brings stability to our lives is obedience to His teachings (Matthew 7:24).

So for a woman to be completely secure in life, she should first be born again and trust alone in Jesus for her eternal salvation. This is true woman's liberation. The truth sets her free.

Other religions treat women as cattle, and they are regularly beaten by their husbands. But in Jesus Christ, women find their first love, forgiveness of sins, honor, and self-respect.

SOUL SEARCH: Is Jesus Christ my first love, and how is His love reflected in my life?

⌒

**Father, I was created with a need to be loved,
and that need has been satisfied in you. Amen.**

THE MOTIVE FOR ATHEISM

He who walks in his uprightness fears the LORD,
but he who is perverse in his ways despises Him.

—PROVERBS 14:2

*H*ere is the motive for atheism. If we have a right standing with God, we will fear Him. However, if we give ourselves to the perversion of pornography, homosexuality, fornication or adultery, or other sins, we will despise God.

The reason we will despise Him is for the same reason criminals despise the police. Criminals will sometimes even kill an officer of the law, not because of who he is but because he stands for righteousness.

Atheists hate God because of His righteous requirements (see Romans 8:7), and the greatest form of contempt they can have for God is to deny His obvious existence.

SOUL SEARCH: How well do I love those who despise what I love?

࿐

Father, I plead with you for the salvation of those who are deceived by the foolishness of atheism. Amen.

April 28

THE SUBTLE WEASEL

In the mouth of a fool is a rod of pride,
but the lips of the wise will preserve them.
—PROVERBS 14:3

*Y*ou can know a foolish man's heart by what comes out of his mouth. Notice that Scripture says that in his mouth is a "rod" of pride. Pride is hard and unbending, and it often inflicts pain to others.

We must have nothing to do with this sort of pride. It is subtle in how it weasels into our hearts, and self-deceiving. Like the proud Pharisee who looked down on the humble publican, pride boasts of its own goodness and looks down on others.

God hates a proud look, and He resists the proud. The Bible even says, "Everyone proud in heart is an abomination to the LORD" (Proverbs 16:5).

SOUL SEARCH: Does what comes out of my mouth exude pride or exemplify the humility of Christ?

◡

**Father, help me to walk with a humble attitude
that always exalts others. Amen.**

April 29

KEEPING IT CLEAN

Where no oxen are, the trough is clean;
but much increase comes by the strength of an ox.
—PROVERBS 14:4

*I*f you want to keep your oxen stall clean, don't put the beasts in it. Today's equivalent would be, "You can't make an omelet without breaking an egg." In other words, if you're going to do something, don't be afraid of messing up.

If you want to share your faith, don't be afraid of messing up. That's how you will become proficient. Every skill you have attained in life came because you were persistent. You learned to crawl, walk, ride a bike, and then drive a car. You were persistent because you wanted to do it, despite not being skilled at the beginning. Apply that principle to reaching a hell-bound world.

SOUL SEARCH: When has the fear of failure held me back from doing exploits for my God? How can I overcome this fear?

**Father, help me to always get up when I fall,
and to trust you through failure. Amen.**

TRUE AND FAITHFUL

A faithful witness does not lie,
but a false witness will utter lies.

—PROVERBS 14:5

The Bible says that lying lips are an abomination to the Lord (Proverbs 12:22), and that all liars will have their part in the lake of fire (Revelation 21:8). Despite the serious nature of this sin, millions lie daily. They think that God is too benevolent to be concerned with such trivialities.

Yet if someone lies as a witness in a court of law, they can end up in prison. We are witnesses of Christ, so we should always be concerned with telling the truth, the whole truth, and nothing but the truth when it comes to the gospel.

God forbid that we should lie about His holiness, the nature of sin, the surety of judgment, or the reality of hell. God help us to be true and faithful witnesses.

SOUL SEARCH: When was the last time I didn't speak the truth, the whole truth, and nothing but the truth?

✑

**Father, never let me deviate from the truth.
Amen.**

May

TRUE WISDOM

A scorner seeks wisdom and does not find it,
but knowledge is easy to him who understands.

—PROVERBS 14:6

The scorner seeks wisdom and doesn't find it. He would no doubt like to have the wisdom to know what stocks to buy or when to invest in the housing market, and attain the wisdom of this world. This earthly wisdom is said in Scripture to be "sensual" and "devilish" (James 3:15).

But a scornful person will never attain godly wisdom until he sets aside his scorn, humbles himself, and seeks the wisdom that comes from above. That is the wisdom that leads to knowledge and produces an understanding of eternal things—and that's what matters most.

SOUL SEARCH: How do I exhibit wisdom from above in my actions?

**Father, please give me the wisdom
that's from above. Amen.**

THE WIZARD

Go from the presence of a foolish man,
when you do not perceive in him the lips of knowledge.

—PROVERBS 14:7

For many years I was friends with an ungodly man who was called "The Wizard." For twelve years, we shared crowds almost daily in Speaker's Corner in my home city in New Zealand. I would preach to the first lunch-hour crowd, he would speak to the second, and sometimes he would let me speak to his crowd.

I surmised that if Jesus could call Judas a friend as Judas betrayed Him with a kiss, I could call this man my friend. And so we swapped birthday and Christmas presents.

Now and then I would stand in his crowd and listen to the fascinating things he said, but then he would suddenly blaspheme the name of God, and I would think of this verse and quickly leave. It's easy to get caught up in a fascination for this world, but it's wise to leave (or turn entertainment off) the second we perceive that such talk would bring the frown of God.

SOUL SEARCH: Do I love my enemies and do good to those who despise me? How does my life show this?

⁓

**Father, help me to be more like my Savior.
Amen.**

May 3

STRAY SHEEP

The wisdom of the prudent is to understand his way,
but the folly of fools is deceit.

—PROVERBS 14:8

We once were like sheep that had gone astray; we had turned every one to his own way. But we're no longer lost. We now belong to the Good Shepherd, who is leading us to eternal life.

It is because of God's amazing grace that we have eternal life through faith in Jesus. Death no longer holds us. If we have trouble expressing such an incredible thought, we're not alone. The apostle Paul spoke of rejoicing with "joy inexpressible" (1 Peter 1:8) and of the "indescribable gift" (2 Corinthians 9:15) when referring to the fact that we have everlasting life in Christ. It will take eternity to comprehend the way God has taken us in.

While we may have trouble articulating such joy, we must still speak the glorious gospel to those who are still in the shadow of death.

SOUL SEARCH: How often am I amazed at God's grace expressed in the cross?

∽

**Father, let me be able to say with the disciples,
"We cannot but speak the things which we have
seen and heard" (Acts 4:20). Amen.**

CONSEQUENTIAL IGNORANCE

Fools mock at sin,
but among the upright there is favor.
—PROVERBS 14:9

A sinner mocking sin is like a child holding a lighted stick of dynamite, laughing as he says that the warning label on the box wasn't true. The child's problem is that he's ignorant of the consequences of his actions. The flicker of the fuse may fascinate, but the repercussions are fearful.

Sin may fascinate the world's eye, but in time it will explode and take to hell all who hold it close to their heart. Sin is never to be mocked or thought of lightly, even by Christians. It will justly damn human beings, and that should break our hearts.

SOUL SEARCH: Which sins do I tend to think of more lightly?

Father, help me to never separate sin and death.
Amen.

THE POWER OF BITTERNESS

The heart knows its own bitterness,
and a stranger does not share its joy.

—PROVERBS 14:10

*M*any things in life can leave us bitter. Friends can turn against us. People we trust can steal our money. Millions become bitter against God, and life itself, when the death of a loved one deals a low blow. Somehow bitterness seems a safe harbor from the storm. But it's really not.

If life has dealt you a low blow, don't let bitterness take you lower. Give it to the Lord and try to forget it. The Bible says, "Forgetting those things which are behind" (Philippians 3:13). Whatever it was, it will steal your joy, and "the joy of the LORD is your strength" (Nehemiah 8:10).

If your heart knows its own bitterness, ask God for a new heart, and let Him turn your mourning into joy.

SOUL SEARCH: Where in my life do I feel bitterness?

~⌒~

**Father, please help me to forgive and forget
anything anyone has done to me. Amen.**

THE DWELLING PLACE

The house of the wicked shall be overthrown:
but the tabernacle of the upright shall flourish.

—PROVERBS 14:11 AKJV

In the battle between good and evil, good will eventually win. We have God's Word on that, and there is nothing more sure.

The "house" of the wicked shall be overthrown, but the "tabernacle" of the upright shall flourish. The tabernacle was the portable dwelling place for God, from the time of the Exodus from Egypt through the conquering of the Promised Land.

Jesus said that the Holy Spirit would come and make His abode within us (John 14:23). God condescended to make His holy presence within the tabernacle of our frail bodies. Christ in us, "the hope of glory" (Colossians 1:27).

SOUL SEARCH: Is Jesus my only hope of glory, or do I tend to place my hope in other things?

**Father, may you and you alone be my hope
and my all. Amen.**

THE WRONG WAY

There is a way that seems right to a man,
but its end is the way of death.
—PROVERBS 14:12

While this "way" that seems right to a man isn't speci-
fied in Scripture, we could probably guess what it is.
I would surmise (based on Scripture and experience) that it's a
belief that we get to heaven by being good. This is the foundation of almost every man-made religion and even the belief of
the irreligious. Even atheists think that Christians believe that
if we are morally good, we will make it to heaven.

However, this belief is destroyed the moment we understand
that when God speaks of "good," He means moral perfection in
thought, word, and deed. If that's the case, no one is good—and
that brings us to the feet of the Savior.

SOUL SEARCH: How well am I able to explain the difference between Christianity and world religions?

**Father, thank you for your everlasting mercy,
without which I would have no hope. Amen.**

May 8

CHASING THE WIND

Even in laughter the heart may sorrow,
and the end of mirth may be grief.

—PROVERBS 14:13

*U*ntil we come to the cross, everything in life is futile. It is like chasing the wind. Love and laughter, every pleasure—even picture-perfect pieces of pizza—are all gone in time and become nothing but a faded memory.

This was Solomon's conclusion after his experiment with life. He cried, "Vanity of vanities. All is vanity" (Ecclesiastes 12:8), all because of one thing that happens to the rich and poor, the wise and foolish. Life has a dead end. Until we come to Jesus Christ, we live in constant dread of death, and even in laughter the heart may sorrow.

Thank God for the unspeakable gift of eternal life that instantly changed futility into purpose, darkness into light, death into life, and mourning into joy.

SOUL SEARCH: Have I come to the conclusion that anything outside the will of God is like chasing the wind? Why?

◌◌

**Father, help me to always seek your guidance,
for without you I can do nothing. Amen.**

THE DIVINE BUTLER

The backslider in heart will be filled with his own ways,
but a good man will be satisfied from above.

—PROVERBS 14:14

We know that we have passed from death to life, so we love the brethren and therefore want to serve them. Like the returning prodigal in Luke 15, we will say to our Father, "Let me be your servant," and to serve God means to serve others.

The false convert, in contrast, has never had that experience. He has never seen his own sins. He's never come to the conclusion that he's a rebel whose heart is deceitfully wicked. And so he looks on God as his servant. To him, his Creator is nothing but a divine butler whose sole reason for existence is to cater to his own selfish will. He has no concern for the lost, and is filled with his own ways rather than the ways of God.

SOUL SEARCH: How much joy do I get from serving others?

Father, show me practical ways I can be
a loving servant. Amen.

May 10

MEDIA BIAS

The simple believes every word,
but the prudent considers well his steps.
—PROVERBS 14:15

*D*on't believe every word you hear from the news media; they often have a bias. Don't believe every word you read in history books; they may have the facts wrong. Don't believe every word you hear from scientists; they are forever changing their minds. And most of all, don't believe every word you hear from a pulpit; there are many false teachers.

Do believe every word in the Bible. It is God breathed, and you can trust every jot and tittle, and so by it you can discern the true and false teacher.

The Scriptures have no bias. They are always right, and they never change. The Bible is the Word of the living God, promising everlasting life to all who trust in His mercy, expressed in Jesus Christ. Believe it with all your heart.

SOUL SEARCH: Have I been as the Bereans, who searched the Scriptures daily to see what the apostle Paul said was true, or do I believe others without question?

⟿

Father, may I always judge what is truth and what is error, from your Word. Amen.

UNWISE WORLD

A wise man fears and departs from evil,
but a fool rages and is self-confident.
—PROVERBS 14:16

There is arguably no greater doctrine that the world finds more offensive than the fear of the Lord. However, they haven't begun to be wise if they don't fear God, because the fear of the Lord is the "beginning" of wisdom.

The Scriptures are filled with admonitions to fear God, not only because He ought to be feared, but because according to Jesus, He has the power to cast the body and soul into hell (Matthew 10:28). That's about as fearful as we could get.

The fear of the Lord is essential for our understanding when it comes to our state before God, because it gives us the desire to depart from our sins. A wise person will fear God and, because of that, depart from evil.

SOUL SEARCH: Does the fear of the Lord govern my thought life, or do I need more fear of Him?

*Father, please teach me what it means
to fear you. Amen.*

May 12

UNBRIDLED ANGER

A quick-tempered man acts foolishly,
and a man of wicked intentions is hated.
—PROVERBS 14:17

Our prisons are full of people who were quick to become angry and have acted foolishly. Perhaps road rage caused a man to kill someone, much to his regret when he came to his senses. Others have hit their wives and ruined marriages, lashed out at the boss and lost jobs, and become angry with friends and destroyed relationships.

The way to prevent anger from possessing us is to have grace toward every other human being. If someone cuts us off on the freeway, perhaps we have been guilty of the same indiscretion. We have all at some time angered our spouse, and we've all been upset with a coworker. Knowledge of our own many sins helps us to extend the grace that God has extended to us.

SOUL SEARCH: What is it that stirs anger in me?

Father, may I only be angry at sin. Amen.

May 13

BELLY SERVERS

The simple inherit folly,
but the prudent are crowned with knowledge.

—PROVERBS 14:18

The Bible says that false teachers deceive the hearts of the simple: "For those who are such do not serve our Lord Jesus Christ, but their own belly, and by smooth words and flattering speech deceive the hearts of the simple" (Romans 16:18). The simple lack the knowledge of God, and so they don't fear Him, nor do they depart from sin.

The law produces the knowledge of sin that leads to salvation. If we don't know we have sinned, we won't see our need of the Savior. But those who have the knowledge that they have sinned against God by violating His perfect law—they find a place of biblical repentance, trust alone in Jesus, and, as kings and priests, are "crowned with knowledge."

SOUL SEARCH: Which of my actions may indicate that my belly is my god? How can I ensure that I serve only the Lord Jesus Christ?

**Father, may my appetite be only for
the things of you. Amen.**

JUSTICE WILL WIN

The evil will bow before the good,
and the wicked at the gates of the righteous.

—PROVERBS 14:19

The evil will bow before the good because God sees the future as the present. He's not bound by time. Justice will defeat injustice, truth will overcome lies, peace will overtake war, love will swallow hatred, and evil will bow before the good.

What a great day for the godly, but a day of terror for sinners, when the sky will roll back and the fury of the Creator will be unleashed upon rebellious sinners. Oh, how they will have remorse that they didn't believe our report!

May God give us the words, the will, the wisdom, and the way to warn every man that almighty God means what He says about evil. May He grant repentance to those who hear and understand the truth of the gospel.

SOUL SEARCH: How often do I think about and cherish the day God saved me?

**Father, may I be so heavenly minded that
I have earthly use. Amen.**

COOL CARS

The poor man is hated even by his own neighbor,
but the rich has many friends.
—PROVERBS 14:20

Rich people have many friends because they have swimming pools, cool cars, and nice boats, and because they go to great restaurants and often give gifts to their friends.

The poor live in bad areas, have older cars, don't have air conditioning, don't eat at fine restaurants, and often ask to borrow money to help pay their bills.

But the poor heard Jesus gladly. They were poor in this world, and they were poor in spirit. The rich are often self-assured and proud, putting money before the love of God. In the light of eternity, we should therefore envy the poor who are rich, and pity the rich who are poor.

SOUL SEARCH: How rich am I in what really matters? In what areas do I want to be rich?

Father, help me to never be attracted by the temporal riches of this world. Amen.

SUPERNATURAL LOVE

He who despises his neighbor sins,
but he who has mercy on the poor, happy is he.
—PROVERBS 14:21

We are commanded by the Scriptures to love all of humanity. If we despise anyone, even if he is our enemy, we are sinning against God. Jesus said to love our enemies and to do good to those who despitefully use us (Matthew 5:44).

This doesn't come easy to sinful human beings. While it's natural to resent people who wrong us, we don't live in the natural world. We live in the supernatural realm, and this is how we are able to love those who hate us.

Not only has the love of God been supernaturally "shed abroad in our hearts" by the Holy Spirit (Romans 5:5 KJV), but we also have Jesus on the cross as our example—where He cried out for His enemies, "Father, forgive them, for they do not know what they do" (Luke 23:34).

SOUL SEARCH: How motivated am I by the words of Jesus?

$\backsim$

**Father, grant me the power to override
natural reactions. Amen.**

THE SNOOZING CONSCIENCE

Do they not go astray who devise evil?
But mercy and truth belong to those who devise good.

—PROVERBS 14:22

Sin seems so right to sin-loving sinners. Like a criminal who finds an unlocked door of a cash-filled bank vault and no one within a mile. Or like the proverbial loose woman who commits adultery and says she has done no wrong. But she has. She has sinned against God and stored up His wrath.

And so has every sinner. His conscience has gone to sleep, and so he, without any fear, devises evil upon his bed. He must be smitten by the law to be shaken out of his delusion so he can see his terrible danger—that his foot hangs over the great precipice of eternity. With the help of God, we must convince him of his error and plead with him to turn before it's too late.

SOUL SEARCH: When was the last time I let my conscience go to sleep?

**Father, let me be awake and wide-eyed
to what is evil. Amen.**

A LITTLE SWEAT

In all labor there is profit,
but idle chatter leads only to poverty.
—PROVERBS 14:23

*T*here is profit in laboring in the fields and in the city. If we are prepared to put our backs to work and sweat a little, there will be rewards.

But there is also a labor that has an eternal reward. Jesus said to look to the fields that are ready to be harvested, but He lamented that the laborers were few (Luke 10:2). They still are. So many in the modern church busy themselves with everything but the backbreaking and sweat-producing labor of evangelism.

Yet that's what we are called to do. We are to engage ourselves in what Charles Spurgeon called an "irksome task." We must apply ourselves to it, because if we profess to have the love of God in us, we can't stand by and let sinners go to hell unwarned.

SOUL SEARCH: How have I been laboring in my evangelistic responsibility? How can I reach out to someone today?

Father, here I am; send me (Isaiah 6:8).
Amen.

RICHES AND TREASURE

The crown of the wise is their riches,
but the foolishness of fools is folly.

—PROVERBS 14:24

*I*f you are trusting in and obeying the words of Jesus, you are like the wise man who built his house on a rock (Matthew 7:24), and your crown is your riches.

The Bible speaks of many different types of riches. We can be rich in faith, rich toward God, and rich in good works. We can have the riches of God's grace and the riches of "full assurance," as well as the riches of God's goodness, and of course the riches of Christ.

Jesus in us is called "treasure in earthen vessels" (2 Corinthians 4:7). The very source of life—the ultimate source of riches dwells within every believer.

So "lay hold on eternal life" (1 Timothy 6:12), keep yourself in the love of God, keep your eyes in His Word and your ears to His voice, and let no man take your crown.

SOUL SEARCH: How have I primed my ears to hear God's voice through His Word today?

✑

**Father, help me lay hold of eternal life.
Amen.**

May 20

IRRATIONAL FEAR

A true witness delivers souls,
but a deceitful witness speaks lies.
—PROVERBS 14:25

*I*f you have been born again, you are a witness of Jesus Christ. Are you therefore witnessing? Do you "deliver souls"? You will if you are a true witness of the Savior's death and resurrection.

Or is your witness stifled by an irrational fear of others? You're not alone if it is. Almost every Christian who wants to be a true and faithful witness has a mountain of fear to conquer.

The way to climb it is to take one step at a time and don't think about how big it is. Start by leaving tracts where people will find them. Then take your next step by handing them out. Then another step the next day, by asking someone if they think there's an afterlife. You can do this! Another word for evangelism is *love*. So don't pray for less fear. Pray for more love.

SOUL SEARCH: Is my irrational fear simply a lack of love? If so, how could I overcome this?

⌒

**Father, let your love in me swallow my fears
so I can speak to the lost. Amen.**

AFTER THE CROSS

In the fear of the LORD there is strong confidence,
and His children will have a place of refuge.

—PROVERBS 14:26

The Bible tells us that it's the fear of the Lord that causes us to depart from evil. But that departure from sin doesn't stop at the cross.

As we cultivate the fear of God in our lives, the result should be sanctification. That means we clean up things that previously didn't bother us. Once we could listen to soft gossip, but as we grew in Christ we refused to listen. Or a word that we once didn't mind saying will now not get past our sanctified lips.

These are signs of spiritual growth, and the result of this will be a clear conscience, confidence in prayer, and a deep assurance that we have a place of refuge in Christ.

SOUL SEARCH: How strong is my confidence when I pray?

**Father, may I never, ever doubt your
impeccable integrity. Amen.**

THE FOUNTAIN OF YOUTH

The fear of the LORD is a fountain of life,
to turn one away from the snares of death.
—PROVERBS 14:27

Shangri-La is a mythological place where people could find the fountain of youth. While the world dreams of eternal youth and yearns for such a place, we have it in Christ. We have this "treasure in earthen vessels" (2 Corinthians 4:7). Our outward man is perishing, but the inward man of eternal youth is being renewed day by day.

Oh, if only the world knew what we have in Christ! If only they knew that through the cross and resurrection of the Son of God, we are free from the snares of death forever, they would gladly give up everything to have Him!

And so, love compels us to take the gospel of everlasting life to them. We must seek God for them, and then seek this dying world for God. And we can do this because we have the promise of His help.

SOUL SEARCH: Is the love of Christ manifest in me? Does it drive me to do God's will daily?

*Father, help me to use every day to glorify you
and to reach the unsaved. Amen.*

WE'LL HONOR THE KING

> In a multitude of people is a king's honor,
> but in the lack of people is the downfall of a prince.
> —PROVERBS 14:28

God has saved us for His glory. One day we will stand around the glorious throne of the King of kings with an innumerable multitude and sing of His majesty and unspeakable glory. We will honor the King.

We can't begin to imagine a thousand rainbows or any sight more glorious than a brilliant sunrise, or music more beautiful than any sound ever heard in this fallen world. That will be the day we see Him face-to-face.

But this world will never know such wonder. They want what comes with the prince of darkness, and they will get the destruction that comes with it. He came to kill, steal, and destroy, and the terrible lake of fire will be his just fate and the fate of all who have willingly followed him. What a fearful thing!

SOUL SEARCH: In what way can I honor the King today?

*Father, don't let me waste my life on
things that don't matter. Amen.*

CONSIDER THE SNAIL AND BE WISE

He who is slow to wrath has great understanding,
but he who is impulsive exalts folly.

—PROVERBS 14:29

We must imitate the snail when it comes to wrath. There is a tornado of destruction waiting to come out of our sinful lips, and impulsivity will open them. This is the nature of our once father, the god of this world.

We know this to be true because the Son of God has come and given us understanding. And so in Him we are slow to wrath. We know that when rage takes hold of a man, he will even destroy what is most dear to him. We therefore hold fury at a distance through Christ who strengthens us against the power of sin.

May we never exalt folly by being impulsive, but instead be swift to hear, slow to speak, and slow to wrath. May we live every day in the fear of God.

SOUL SEARCH: When was the last time I exalted folly?

Father, keep eternity in my eyes. Amen.

THE POWER OF EMOTION

A sound heart is life to the body,
but envy is rottenness to the bones.
—PROVERBS 14:30

Our fearfully and wonderfully made bodies are extremely complex. The Bible, nearly three thousand years ago, spoke of psychosomatic illnesses. Envy and other human emotions can affect the health of the human body. Envy has the bad bedfellows of covetousness, jealousy, and hatred. We see this so clearly in the case of King Saul and David. The king envied the praise given to David. He coveted it, became jealous of it, and hated him because of it, which then led to his attempt to kill him.

So don't let envy through the door. Guard your heart with all diligence from this subtle sin, because it will seek to take possession of the whole house.

SOUL SEARCH: What things do I envy in secret?

**Search my heart today, O God. Help me
to be free of envy. Amen.**

THE PREY OF THE RICH

He who oppresses the poor reproaches his Maker,
but he who honors Him has mercy on the needy.

—PROVERBS 14:31

It's the rich who oppress the poor, perhaps because the poor don't have the means to oppress anyone. The wealthy so often collect their wealth by squeezing what wealth the poor have and making it their own.

Thomas Jefferson said, "Experience demands that man is the only animal which devours his own kind, for I can apply no milder term to the general prey of the rich on the poor." Communism seeks to spread the wealth to the poor, making it communal. The problem is that the rich aren't too excited about having their wealth spread. So in history, communism has killed the rich to get their riches.

The Christian instead has love enough to have mercy on the poor, and cheerfully gives when he sees a need. In doing so, he honors God.

SOUL SEARCH: How cheerfully do I give of my time and resources?

**Father, let me be a giver and not a taker.
Amen.**

DRIVEN BY THE DEVIL

The wicked is banished in his wickedness,
but the righteous has a refuge in his death.

—PROVERBS 14:32

Those who give themselves to sin give the steering wheel to the devil. They are driven away in their wickedness and are destined for a head-on collision with God's law. Their understanding is darkened, and they have no idea that they are on the road to hell.

The righteous, however, have been born again and have a glorious hope in their death. This hope of everlasting life is both sure and steadfast and an anchor to the soul, all because Jesus Christ suffered and died, then rose again on the third day.

By the grace of God, He conquered the grave. It was not possible that death could hold Him. When we trust in the Savior alone, we belong to Him, and because of that it is not possible that death can hold us either.

SOUL SEARCH: How often do I truly appreciate the cost of my redemption?

⁄○

**Father, help me to glory in the cross of Jesus Christ
(Galatians 6:14). Amen.**

May 28

NO PANIC

Wisdom rests in the heart of him who has understanding,
but what is in the heart of fools is made known.

—PROVERBS 14:33

*W*isdom rests in the heart, and it has a rest that isn't disturbed. It doesn't panic in a storm, and it isn't fearful of the future or plagued by the past. This is because it keeps its mind stayed on God. Wisdom has the understanding that whatever trials come her way, they come only by the permissive will of almighty God.

Wisdom was personified in and through the life of Jesus of Nazareth. From His humble sitting at the feet of the teachers of the law as a young boy, to His agonizing submission to the will of His Father in the garden of Gethsemane, we see the wisdom of God manifest in His perfect life.

Love Him and you love wisdom. Imitate Him and you are wise. Listen to His Word and you listen to wisdom—and in doing so, you love your own soul.

SOUL SEARCH: Do I tend to panic in a storm, or am I sure in Christ?

**Father, help me to trust your wisdom
in stormy trials. Amen.**

May 29

COCKROACHES IN THE NIGHT

Righteousness exalts a nation,
but sin is a reproach to any people.
—PROVERBS 14:34

Righteousness lifts a nation out of the darkness. It makes it like a city set upon a hill, shining with light.

But sinners love darkness rather than light. Like cockroaches in the night, they build their reproachful city on the dunghill of sin. They feed on the shame of pornography, adultery, fornication, homosexuality, rebellion, and blasphemy, and demand the legal right to kill their own offspring in the womb.

It's foreign to our sin-loving nature to love righteousness. This is why we must plead with Him to extend His mercy. Without it, this shameless world will be justly damned by His law.

May God use us to reach the lost with the gospel of grace that saves sinners from hell.

SOUL SEARCH: At what times in my life have I strayed from a love of righteousness?

⟲

Father, never let me stray. Amen.

THE FAVOR OF THE KING

The king's favor is toward a wise servant,
but his wrath is against him who causes shame.

—PROVERBS 14:35

In Matthew 24:45, Jesus spoke of a "wise servant." That's what we are in Christ. We have the King's favor because of the cross of Calvary.

At our conversion, God Himself clothed us in the righteousness of Jesus Christ, and now we can come boldly before the throne of grace and have His smile. In a moment of time, we moved from being under God's fierce wrath for our sins, into His favor because we are in Christ.

How could we ever find ourselves in the valley of depression when we understand this great truth? May we always stand on the mountaintop of praise to God for His great goodness and His everlasting mercy toward us.

SOUL SEARCH: Am I seen by others as a wise servant, or have I caused shame?

Father, let this day be a day that I exercise godly wisdom in all that I think, say, and do. Amen.

HOW TO PUT OUT THE FLAME

A soft answer turns away wrath,
but a harsh word stirs up anger.

—PROVERBS 15:1

If you're a Christian and you're faithfully sharing the gospel, deposit this verse in the safety of your memory bank. Someday you will need to make a quick withdrawal on its wisdom. Someone is going to be angered by the truth, and you will need to answer their wrath softly. A soft answer is like a bucket of cool water on hot flames.

It is also wise to divert wrath. I was once approached by a very angry young lady who was deeply offended by my preaching. It seemed as though she was about to hit me, so I said, "That's a nice sweater." She immediately took her eyes off me and looked down at her colorful sweater, then smiled.

So keep being faithful, bold, and gentle. Uncompromisingly preach the truth in love, because your labor is never in vain.

SOUL SEARCH: When was the last time my fuse was short? How can I avoid harsh words today?

⁓

**Father, let me have a soft answer in contention.
Amen.**

June

June 1

TAMING THE TONGUE

The tongue of the wise uses knowledge rightly,
but the mouth of fools pours forth foolishness.

—PROVERBS 15:2

Our wild and twitching tongues are quick to use knowledge wrongly (gossip is sweet to the unsanctified heart). But the tongue of the learned has been broken, saddled, and brought into the obedience of what is right and good. The tongue of the wise is used in the saving of souls. It is sanctified and ready for the Master's use.

The Christian uses knowledge rightly to show sinners they have violated the moral law and therefore need God's mercy. He is mindful of the lost, and uses the law to bring the knowledge of sin, to show sin to be exceedingly wrong.

May we never use our mouths to pour forth foolishness. Instead, may they be used to tell dying sinners of the Savior's undying love so evidently displayed on the cross of Calvary two thousand years ago.

SOUL SEARCH: How do I react to gossip?

**Father, teach me to turn a deaf ear
to all gossip. Amen.**

MIND-BLOWING THOUGHTS

The eyes of the LORD are in every place,
keeping watch on the evil and the good.

—PROVERBS 15:3

When the Bible speaks of God having eyes, it is an anthropomorphic statement. It doesn't mean that He has physical eyes. It means that God can see—which makes sense, seeing that He is the maker of the billions of eyes in human beings, as well as the eyes of cats, dogs, horses, cows, frogs, birds, fleas, and fish.

And His eyes are in every place (2 Chronicles 16:9; Proverbs 15:3). "Every" means that He sees us from above and from below. He sees the thoughts that pass through our minds; He sees the darkness as light, into the infinitude of space, as well as into the bottom soil on the floor of the deepest ocean. He also sees in the middle of every rock, and even the atoms that make up the heart of our fiery sun.

Such thoughts are too much for any human mind, and leave those who entertain such thoughts in an attitude of quiet worship.

SOUL SEARCH: How am I living in the light of God's omnipresence?

Father, help me to always be conscious
of your presence. Amen.

THE TREE OF LIFE

A wholesome tongue is a tree of life,
but perverseness in it breaks the spirit.

—PROVERBS 15:4

We lost the tree of life in the garden of Eden, and it was won back in another garden—the garden of Gethsemane, where our redemption was made sure. The moment Jesus uttered the agonizing words "Not my will, but Yours, be done" (Luke 22:42), our salvation was sealed. His word was enough. It was as good as done.

A wholesome tongue indeed preaches the gospel of everlasting life to dying sinners—that God made a way back to the tree of life. The suffering death of the perfect Lamb of God meant that the angels could put down the "flaming sword which turned every way, to guard the way to the tree of life" (Genesis 3:24).

The flaming sword of eternal justice was satisfied the moment Jesus cried, "It is finished!" (John 19:30). The debt had been paid. Access to everlasting life had been made through His precious blood.

SOUL SEARCH: Is my word enough when I give it, or have my past actions caused some to doubt me?

⌒

**Father, help me to keep my word and
exemplify your nature. Amen.**

INTUITIVE LOVE

A fool despises his father's instruction,
but he who receives correction is prudent.

—PROVERBS 15:5

A father has an intuitive love for his son. He wants what's best for his own flesh and blood. He teaches him that fire burns, water drowns, and speed kills. Only a fool doesn't listen to advice that is provoked by love and given for good.

In Christ, God can look on us with love and be well pleased with what He sees. Our sins are not only forgiven; they are also washed away, and we are clothed in the righteousness of Christ. We can now call the One with whom we were once enemies "Father."

And so what fools we would be to not listen to His instructions! We should therefore daily soak our souls in His Instruction Book, the Bible, for "all Scripture is given by inspiration of God, and is profitable for doctrine, for reproof, for correction, for instruction in righteousness, that the man of God may be complete, thoroughly equipped for every good work" (2 Timothy 3:16–17).

SOUL SEARCH: How have I personalized the Bible by listening to the instruction of the Scriptures?

*Father, please put a divine hunger in my soul
for your precious Word. Amen.*

June 5

THE LIFE FORCE

In the house of the righteous there is much treasure,
but in the revenue of the wicked is trouble.

—PROVERBS 15:6

"*We* have this treasure in earthen vessels" (2 Corinthians 4:7). The life force has made His abode in human habitations. Within this earthly house, this weak clay tabernacle, God (who is the source of eternal life) has condescended to make His abode.

We have been saved from death, sealed by God, and destined for eternal glory. How can we begin to explain such wonderful truths to a spiritually blind world? It would be easier to explain a rainbow to a blind man who has never seen light. He has no idea of what blue, green, or red are, and we have no way to explain them to him. He needs light.

And so the blind sinner needs light, and we can help give it to him by sharing the light of God's law (to bring the knowledge of sin). Then when he is humble, we can give him the light of the glorious gospel of Christ.

SOUL SEARCH: When was the last time I forgot to be dependent on God?

Father, you are my very breath of life. Amen.

June 6

LOWER-FLOOR FIRE

The lips of the wise disperse knowledge,
but the heart of the fool does not do so.
—PROVERBS 15:7

As Christians, we are like someone in the early hours of the morning on the top floor of a high-rise building. A fire has broken out on a lower floor, and it's only a matter of time until many lives are lost if they aren't awakened from their sleep and told how to exit safely. We know how to get out of the building, and so we go from room to room, passing on the knowledge that will save their lives. We quickly awaken those who are asleep, and then we tell them the way of escape.

We awaken sleeping sinners using the moral law (which brings the knowledge of sin), and then we show them the way of escape—through the good news of the gospel. "How shall we escape if we neglect so great a salvation?" (Hebrews 2:3).

SOUL SEARCH: How important is it to me to reach the lost?

Father, let your love in me stir a zeal in me
to reach the lost. Amen.

THE BASIS OF RELIGION

The sacrifice of the wicked is an abomination to the LORD,
but the prayer of the upright is His delight.

—PROVERBS 15:8

*T*his is the basis of all religions except for Christianity: people can merit everlasting life by their own self-sacrifice. Guilt stirs them to try to make up for their sins by being good. They have sinned, therefore if they provide a payment they will be made right with God. They will be "justified." They erroneously think that they can balance the scales.

But that won't work even in a criminal court. What would happen if a defendant claimed, "Judge, I did rape the woman, but I have done a lot of good things, and I give money to charities"? The judge would still take only his crime into account. Anything good he has done would be irrelevant.

But our "good" works aren't good at all. They are attempts to bribe the Judge of the universe, and He will not be bribed. The sacrifice of the wicked is an abomination to Him.

SOUL SEARCH: How would I define "a person of prayer"? Am I one?

Father, may prayer be as natural to me
as breathing. Amen.

June 8

THE WAY OF ADAM

The way of the wicked is an abomination to the LORD,
but He loves him who follows righteousness.

—PROVERBS 15:9

*B*efore we came to the Savior, we were like sheep that had gone astray. We had turned "every one, to his own way" (Isaiah 53:6). We took the way Adam took when he hid from God in the garden of Eden. It was the way of rebellion to our Creator, and it brought upon us His just wrath (John 3:36).

But by the grace of our God, the Good Shepherd searched for us, found us, and carried us back to the fold. We no longer go our own sinful way because we are no longer our own. We have been bought with a price—the precious blood of Christ (such is the love of God for us)—and He now leads us in the paths of righteousness for His name's sake (Psalm 23:3).

SOUL SEARCH: How often do I thirst for righteousness? What am I thirsty for today?

◦◦◦

**Father, lead me in the path
of righteousness. Amen.**

June 9

LIONS' DENS
AND RED SEAS

Harsh discipline is for him who forsakes the way,
and he who hates correction will die.

—PROVERBS 15:10

ebrews 12:5–6 tells us that God corrects and chastens those He loves. No trial is enjoyable, but God allows them to come our way for our good. Lions' dens and Red Seas bring us to our knees, but we come out of them saying with the psalmist, "It is good for me that I have been afflicted, that I may learn Your statues" (Psalm 119:71). These trials are good for us because all things work together for the good of those who love God and are called according to His purposes (Romans 8:28).

Although it's not an easy thing to do, we must therefore learn to give thanks in and for these trials. So if you are in one today, offer God the sacrifice of praise. Strengthen your feeble knees and then lift up your holy hands to Him in worship. Praise Him anyway, let the joy of the Lord be your strength (Nehemiah 8:10), and may God deliver you quickly.

SOUL SEARCH: Is harsh discipline difficult for me, or do I welcome God's correction?

*Father, help me to see your hand in daily trials
and your promise to work them for my good. Amen.*

June 10

UNENDING FEAR

Hell and Destruction are before the LORD;
so how much more the hearts of the sons of men.

—PROVERBS 15:11

The reality of hell is forever before the omniscient eyes of God. He sees the terrible destruction of those who die in their sins.

As Christians we also need to be ever mindful of the existence of hell. Have you ever woken from a nightmare thankful that you awoke and were able to shake off the fear? Imagine that fear being unending.

Think often of the fate of the unsaved. The Bible warns, "But to those who are self-seeking and do not obey the truth, but obey unrighteousness—indignation and wrath" (Romans 2:8). Such thoughts should take our breath away and bring us to our knees. Paul said, "Knowing, therefore, the terror of the Lord, we persuade men" (2 Corinthians 5:11).

SOUL SEARCH: How often do I think of the fate of the lost?

~

Father, help me to shun selfishness. Amen.

SCORN AND PRIDE

A scoffer does not love one who corrects him,
nor will he go to the wise.

—PROVERBS 15:12

Scorn and pride go hand in hand. The scoffer sits himself on high moral ground and looks condescendingly on the godly. The foolishness of the gospel is an offense to him. His mind is set on the things of the flesh and his wisdom is from below: "sensual, devilish" (James 3:15 KJV). Such a proud peacock isn't easy to love, but we must love him and be concerned for his salvation.

He won't come to the light, so we must take the light to him, take courage, and reprove him for sinning against God. Unless he repents and trusts in Jesus, he will die in his sins and end up in hell. How frightening for him!

May God give us a love that doesn't seek the approval of this scornful world, so we may warn them no matter how they respond to us.

SOUL SEARCH: How often do I make fear a matter of prayer?

Father, may the love of God swallow my fears, so I can persuade men and women to trust the Savior. Amen.

GIVING UP THE REINS

A merry heart makes a cheerful countenance,
but by sorrow of the heart the spirit is broken.

—PROVERBS 15:13

*W*hen a wild horse is "broken," it's the spirit that is broken. The animal's individual character and its energy remain. It simply becomes harnessed and therefore useful. The horse now submits to the rider and moves in any direction he wills.

Trials break our spirit. They make us sorrowful. They bring us to a point of handing God the reins of our rebellious lives, and saying, "Not my will, but Yours, be done" (Luke 22:42). Our individual character and our energy remain, but they are now harnessed for the Master's use. When God says, "This is the way," that's the way we turn, because we are no longer our own. We have presented our bodies as living sacrifices, knowing that "the sacrifices of God are … a broken and a contrite heart" (Psalm 51:17).

SOUL SEARCH: In what area do I need to give up the reins and say, "Not my will, but yours be done?" to the Lord?

⌁

**Father, I give you my broken and contrite heart.
Do as you will in my life. Amen.**

June 13

THE DOOR OF UNDERSTANDING

The heart of him who has understanding seeks knowledge,
but the mouth of fools feeds on foolishness.

—PROVERBS 15:14

What do we hunger for? Do we hunger after righteousness, or does our mouth feed on foolishness? This sinful world certainly serves up foolishness and encourages us to indulge.

But the heart of him who understands seeks knowledge. The Son of God has come and given us understanding. It was by the grace of God that we entered the kingdom through the door of understanding. Our minds were once darkened, and we were alienated from the life of God because of the ignorance that was in us.

But now we seek the knowledge of God. We desire to grow in Him through the power of His Spirit and through the light of His Word. We are no longer in darkness, feeding on foolishness, deceived by this world.

SOUL SEARCH: When was the last time I wasted my time on foolishness?

Father, help me to use my time wisely. Amen.

THE CONTINUAL FEAST

All the days of the afflicted are evil,
but he who is of a merry heart has a continual feast.
—PROVERBS 15:15

Some people are born with a merry heart. They seem to always have a sparkle in their eye and are upbeat about everything. They are born that way because joy is in their genes.

But when we are born again, we can determine whether or not we have joy. We can give ourselves a merry heart using something that is available to all of us—faith. If someone promised to give you a million dollars, you would have a merry heart the very moment you believed. If you didn't believe, you would have no joy.

God's Word has promises that are to be desired more than fine gold. Believe them with all your heart, and have a continual feast.

SOUL SEARCH: How much of me does God have? What would it take to give all of myself to Him?

Father, show me if I am unconsciously holding back
in any area of my life. Amen.

June 15

HOW TO NOT FEAR GOD

Better is little with the fear of the LORD,
than great treasure with trouble.

—PROVERBS 15:16

There are many promises in Scripture for those who fear the Lord. Such fear is both the beginning of wisdom and the motivation for sin-loving sinners to let go of their beloved sins. And nothing dissipates that fear like idolatry.

To believe that God is all-loving or too good to create hell is to make up a nonexistent god and violate the first and the second of the Ten Commandments. However, those who embrace the biblical revelation of our Creator will know the fear of Lord and find the knowledge of God. Like the psalmist, they will say, "My flesh trembles for fear of You" (Psalm 119:120), and like Paul, will proclaim, "Knowing, therefore, the terror of the Lord, we persuade men" (2 Corinthians 5:11).

SOUL SEARCH: How do I feel about the fear of God? Is it an uncomfortable thought?

Father, remove idolatry far from me. Amen.

June 16

MIGNON ON THE ROCKS

Better is a dinner of herbs where love is,
than a fatted calf with hatred.
—PROVERBS 15:17

*B*etter to eat lettuce and have a good marriage, than filet mignon and have a marriage on the rocks. Complex counsel is often poured onto problem marriages in an effort to save them, when the Bible gives simple ingredients to make them work: "Husbands, love your wives, just as Christ also loved the church and gave Himself for it" (Ephesians 5:25), and "Wives, submit to your own husbands" (v. 22).

A marriage works when self is left outside the door. Then hatred can't get in. In reality, it's not the marriage that's the problem; it's selfishness. It's a lack of the fruit the Spirit. Where there is no love, there is no salvation. Many who profess Christ don't possess Christ.

SOUL SEARCH: Who is on my throne? Is it self, or is it God?

⁄◦

Father, may I this day reckon my sinful self dead in Christ (Romans 6:11). Amen.

HEART CONDITION

A wrathful man stirs up strife,
but he who is slow to anger allays contention.
—PROVERBS 15:18

We must never forget that we have an enemy who came to kill, steal, and destroy (John 10:10). He seeks to put a match to short fuses and stir up strife that kills marriages, steals our joy, and destroys relationships.

It's thought provoking to consider that circumstances don't cause anger; instead, they reveal it. How we react when cut off on a freeway, or when a coworker steps on our toes, or when we don't get our own way at home reveals our heart condition. If we lack grace toward others and react in anger, it's probably because we have never caught a glimpse of our own sinfulness.

Knowledge of our personal moral shortcomings keeps pride at bay. "I'm right!" is the fuel that drives the vehicle of wrath, but humility puts a foot on the brake and appeases strife.

SOUL SEARCH: Am I a peacemaker, or do I struggle with wrath?

**Father, make me a peacemaker between
sinful humanity and you. Amen.**

AVOID THIS EXPERIENCE

The way of the lazy man is like a hedge of thorns,
but the way of the upright is a highway.
—PROVERBS 15:19

No sane person needs to be warned about going through a hedge of thorns. To do so would be a painful experience. The way of the lazy man is like a hedge of thorns. He can't be trusted to carry out any task. Having to deal with him is a painful experience, and one that is best avoided.

May we never be slothful, but be diligent with everything to which we put our hand, especially the sobering task of evangelism. It is difficult work, but it's also the lifeblood of the church. It is a way that's been made plain by the Great Commission and by the path set before us by the early church in the book of Acts.

May we never be a hedge of thorns when it comes to this high and holy calling of reaching out to dying sinners.

SOUL SEARCH: Do I ever get lazy, or is laziness repulsive to me?

Father, may I be one who is steadfast in
my labors for you. Amen.

MAKING GOD GLAD

A wise son makes a glad father,
but a foolish man despises his mother.

—PROVERBS 15:20

The moment you and I put our trust in Jesus, not only were our sins forgiven, but God became our Father. We were translated out of the kingdom of darkness into the kingdom of light. We were adopted into His family through the new birth, and—wonder of wonders—we can make our Father glad. He can look at us in Christ and say, "This is my beloved child, in whom I am well pleased" (see Matthew 3:16–17). The Bible even says that God rejoices over us with singing (Zephaniah 3:17).

So be wise and always do the things that please Him. Live in righteousness, feed on the Word daily, pray without ceasing, confess your sins regularly, and reach out to the lost. Always be assured that you have His smile because you are in Christ.

SOUL SEARCH: Do all my daily decisions please my Father? What decisions should I no longer make?

Father, may my highest aim be to please you.
Amen.

THE JOY OF LAUGHTER

Folly is joy to him who is destitute of discernment,
but a man of understanding walks uprightly.

—PROVERBS 15:21

A merry heart does good like a medicine, and merriment finds itself expressed in laughter, which is good for the soul.

I have found from experience that those who are close to God know how to laugh. They have a good sense of humor and enjoy a good laugh. Sadly, much of the world's humor is unclean. They call it "adult" humor, but it is more aptly called "gutter" humor. This is a filthy ditch that a Christian should never enter.

Other humor may not be filthy, but it is nothing but foolishness. Those who lack godly wisdom are delighted by childish stupidity, but those who have wisdom from God walk above it.

SOUL SEARCH: Does foolishness ever make me laugh, or do I always walk above it?

⟡

**Father, may I only laugh at what would bring
a smile to heaven. Amen.**

RIDING HIGH IN APRIL

Without counsel, plans go awry,
but in the multitude of counselors they are established.

—PROVERBS 15:22

Life is filled with continual disappointments. We ride high in April but are shot down in May. These are dis-appointments—dismissed appointments. They promise but don't deliver.

But there is a way for us to keep these disappointments at a minimum: always seek godly advice. It costs us nothing but time to listen to counsel, and words given may provide another perspective that saves us a lot of pain. We should search out the wise of heart for any decision that has the potential to change our lives for the better or the worse.

We have God's Word warning us that without counsel, what we are proposing will end up disappointing us. But if we ask advice from those who are wise, our purposes will be established.

SOUL SEARCH: Do I seek counsel from others, or is God's Word my final word?

⟜⟝

**Father, let your will be done in all things
that pertain to my life. Amen.**

A GOOD ANSWER

A man has joy by the answer of his mouth,
and a word spoken in due season, how good it is!

—PROVERBS 15:23

It's a great feeling to get praised for a good answer, whether it's given in school by a teacher, at work by a boss, or at home by a spouse. How much better then is the feeling when we give biblically correct answers to life's many and complex questions. What a joy it is to tell dying sinners that Jesus Christ has abolished death, and that the new birth takes us out of darkness into light.

If one word in due season is good, how much better it is to "preach the word … in season and out of season" (2 Timothy 4:2). That is a source of joy unspeakable for those who have the honor of preaching the glad tidings of good news.

SOUL SEARCH: When was the last time I encouraged someone with good advice?

**Father, let my words always build up
and not destroy. Amen.**

LOVE WARNS

The way of life winds upward for the wise,
that he may turn away from hell below.

—PROVERBS 15:24

*T*he accusation of the skeptic is that we use the threat of hell to control the weak-minded. That may be true of some religions that hold their power because they control the masses, but the second the skeptic finds himself in hell, he will know that we only warned of it because we loved him.

Do we ever weep as we pray for the lost? Dry eyes and hard hearts go hand in hand. How can we profess to have the love of God in our hearts if we don't plead with the unsaved to repent and turn to the Savior? And how can we do that with any passion if we don't care?

Thoughts of heaven above are pleasant, while thoughts of hell beneath aren't at all desirable. But we must force ourselves to think of both. Without the unpleasant thoughts about hell, we will never plead with any urgency.

SOUL SEARCH: When was the last time I shed tears for the unsaved? For whom does God want to give me a heart of compassion?

**Father, may I weep over the "Jerusalem"
of this world. Amen.**

SHIFTING SAND

The LORD will destroy the house of the proud,
but He will establish the boundary of the widow.
—PROVERBS 15:25

*O*ur hearts should break for the godless widow. The love of her life has been taken by death, and now she lives in an empty home filled with painful memories. It is because she has ignored the sayings of Jesus that she built her house on shifting sand, and when the storms came, it all came crashing down.

But the woman who obeys God's words builds her house on rock. She has the consolation of the gospel and the knowledge that all of her life experiences are working for her good (Romans 8:28). The godly woman makes sure her trust is foremost in God, and she has made Jesus her first love. She knows that He will establish the boundary of her life.

SOUL SEARCH: How do I show my care for widows?

**Father, make the needs of others, especially widows,
known to me. Amen.**

GOD'S NOT DEAF

The thoughts of the wicked are an abomination to the LORD,
but the words of the pure are pleasant.

—PROVERBS 15:26

*H*e who made the eye can also see. He who made the ear is not deaf. And the One who created the human mind sees it at work and hears its thoughts. Think about it. The omniscience of God goes into the deepest recesses of the brain of every creature He made. "Such knowledge is too wonderful for me. It is high, I cannot attain it," says the psalmist (Psalm 139:6).

But the fearful thought is that God sees human thought from the point of His holiness and equates lust to adultery and hatred to murder. Our thoughts before we came to Christ were an abomination to Him. They were extremely detestable. But in Christ, we have been washed and given the mind of Christ. May our thoughts today be filled with love for God and gratitude to Him for His unspeakable gift.

SOUL SEARCH: When was the last time I meditated on the breathtaking greatness of God?

⌁

**Father, take off my blinders and help me to see
the exceeding greatness of your power. Amen.**

June 26

SUBTLE POISON

He who is greedy for gain troubles his own house,
but he who hates bribes will live.

—PROVERBS 15:27

Ambition is greed in disguise. Shakespeare warned:

I charge thee, fling away ambition:
By that sin fell the angels; how can man, then,
The image of his Maker, hope to win by it?

Ambition and greed take husbands from wives and fathers from children. They trouble the home.

Greed can even disguise itself as love. The Bible says that the love of money is the root of all evil (1 Timothy 6:10). Don't let the poison of greed come near. It promises life and freedom but will put a noose around your neck. Just ask Judas.

So the way to keep your heart from greed is to keep your hand on an open wallet. Give money away regularly. It will do your soul good.

SOUL SEARCH: Am I a candidate for greed? Why?

Father, let me be a cheerful giver. Amen.

ROOMY LIFEBOAT

The heart of the righteous studies how to answer,
but the mouth of the wicked pours forth evil.

—PROVERBS 15:28

The righteous are those who have been made right with God by His amazing grace—through faith alone in Jesus. They are the saved.

We are like the survivors of the *Titanic*, sitting in the roomy lifeboat of the Savior, while all around us people are sinking without hope into an icy grave. How can we not do all we can to help them get into the lifeboat?

We study how to answer their questions. We want to remove every stumbling block between them and their salvation. We learn how to answer about disease, suffering, and death. We study so that we know to do what Jesus did when it came to reaching out to the unsaved. We give God's law to the proud and His amazing grace to the humble.

SOUL SEARCH: How do I answer the difficult questions asked by the unsaved?

**Father, teach me how to wisely and lovingly
speak to this sinful world. Amen.**

GOD'S DELIBERATE DEAFNESS

The LORD is far from the wicked,
but he hears the prayer of the righteous.

—PROVERBS 15:29

Atheists often mock the very thought of God, saying that there is no evidence for His existence. But they inherently know that He exists because God has revealed Himself to them through creation. Romans 1:20 says that creation is clearly seen, so they are without excuse.

However, they are not aware of His immediate presence, as are the godly. This is because He separates Himself from them because of their sin. He knows them from far off, and His ear is deaf to their prayers until they seek Him with a humble heart.

Those who have humbled themselves and have been saved by His grace know that He is faithful to hear their prayers.

SOUL SEARCH: Have I humbled my heart, or do I still struggle with pride?

**Father, help me to always see myself in truth.
Amen.**

June 29

FAT BONES

The light of the eyes rejoices the heart,
and a good report makes the bones healthy.

—PROVERBS 15:30

If any people on earth should have a rejoicing heart and healthy bones, it's Christians. Our eyes have been enlightened to see eternity, and there is no better report than the glorious gospel of Jesus Christ.

Our heart now bursts with "joy unspeakable" (1 Peter 1:8 KJV) because the sacrifice that Jesus offered the Father satisfied the demands of eternal justice. This was confirmed by His resurrection. It was impossible for death to hold Him, and in that moment of time that He rose, chains fell off for every damned sinner who would come to the Savior in repentance and faith.

May the "joy of the Lord" (Nehemiah 8:10) be the strength that we need to take this glorious gospel to those who sit without hope in the dark shadow of death.

SOUL SEARCH: How often do I rejoice that Jesus has saved me from death?

**Father, let my heart burst with joy unspeakable.
Amen.**

ABIDING AMONG THE WISE

The ear that hears the rebukes of life
will abide among the wise.

—PROVERBS 15:31

Have you heard the rebukes of life? Are you abiding in Christ? Then you are abiding among the wise, and the Scriptures say that the wise win souls. Of course it is God who saves souls, but with His help we can win the lost with words, specifically the words of the gospel. It is "the power of God to salvation" (Romans 1:16).

The gospel of Jesus Christ is the rebuke of life, and they who listen are wise. You and I can play some part in causing people to listen to and understand the gospel. Pray that today God uses you to speak a word or give out a tract, and be faithful in what He's called you to do.

SOUL SEARCH: Am I about my Father's business (Luke 2:49), or am I about my own?

⌐∽

**Father, let me be busy for your kingdom this day.
Amen.**

July

July 1

WANTING THE BEST

He who disdains instruction despises his own soul,
but he who heeds rebuke gets understanding.

—PROVERBS 15:32

The Bible often uses hyperbole to make an important point. It contrasts love with hatred for the sake of emphasis.

No man in his right mind despises his own soul. He intuitively wants happiness and therefore wants the best for himself. But if he is so proud that he refuses to learn from others, he may as well despise himself because he will suffer for his foolishness.

And there are many people like that. They refuse instruction in righteousness from the Word of God, and those who do so will lose their precious lives. Jesus said, "What profit is it to a man if he gains the whole world, and loses his own soul?" (Matthew 16:26).

SOUL SEARCH: What instructions in the Bible have I shunned?

∽

Father, help me to be quick to do your will today.
Amen.

July 2

HONOR FROM GOD

The fear of the Lord is the instruction of wisdom,
and before honor is humility.

—PROVERBS 15:33

If you want God to honor you in Christ, humble yourself and serve others. When I'm asked what someone should do to be trusted with an international ministry, I say to serve others. Humility does that. It washes feet. It also washes dishes.

Whenever I was a guest speaker at a Bible school or camp, I would always make my way to the kitchen after dinner and help with the dishes. Sometimes crowds of Christians would come and stare, as though it was unusual to see a guest speaker doing such lowly tasks, but I thought it should be the norm.

So, do the lowly tasks and watch God honor His Word—and you.

SOUL SEARCH: When was the last time I performed a lowly task? What is one task I could perform regularly?

**Father, help me to see the lowliest task
as being highly honorable. Amen.**

DIRECTED STEPS

The preparations of the heart belong to man,
but the answer of the tongue is from the LORD.

—PROVERBS 16:1

*M*ay it always be the case that God directs our steps. None who love the Lord want to stray from His will, so it's consoling for us to know that even though we make our plans, God in His faithfulness will cause the outcome to work for our good (Romans 8:28).

But more than that, if we prepare our hearts to share the gospel with the unsaved, we can also be assured of His help. Most of us who share our faith have heard ourselves witness of the truth and then wonder about the origin of our thoughts. We then conclude that we had the help of the Holy Spirit. We made preparations in our hearts, but God put words on our tongue.

John Wesley said of this verse: "Men can neither think nor speak wisely and well without Divine assistance."*

SOUL SEARCH: Is my heart ready to speak with the unsaved? If not, what do I need to do to prepare myself?

⌇◦

Father, make me as bold as a lion. Amen.

---

* John Wesley's Explanatory Notes (Proverbs 16:1), Christianity.com, http://www.christianity.com/bible/commentary.php?com=wes&b=20&c=16.

OUR HIDDEN MOTIVES

All the ways of a man are clean in his own eyes,
but the LORD weighs the spirits.
—PROVERBS 16:2

When theist Thomas Edison said, "We don't know one-millionth of one percent about anything,"* he understated the matter. We boast of our knowledge, our inventions, and our technological advancements, but compared to the mind of God, the human mind is infinitely less than utterly pathetic. We know nothing at all.

How could God weigh spirits? How could He see our hidden motives and make a perfect judgment? How could He create our brains to think, reason, and imagine, with the string of subconscious thoughts that continually speak to us and frame further thoughts?

The answer is that we haven't the slightest idea about this, let alone do we understand the eternal, the infinite, and the invisible.

SOUL SEARCH: In what do I see Him who is invisible?

ᴄ⁄ᴐ

**Father, help me to contrast your greatness
with my weakness so I lean fully on you. Amen.**

---

* "Famous Quotations from Thomas Edison," Edison Innovation Foundation, http://www.thomasedison.org/index.php/education/edison-quotes/.

July 5

THE COMFORT ZONE

Commit your works to the LORD,
and your thoughts will be established.

—PROVERBS 16:3

*T*his verse is very meaningful to me. It jumped out as I was reading my Bible way back in 1977, as I was considering writing my first book. I was hesitant because writing didn't come easily to me when I was in school. But I certainly had a strong conviction to write it, because five of my surfing buddies had died because of drug abuse.

I settled on the title *My Friends Are Dying!* and then stood on this wonderful promise, stayed up nights, and finished the entire book in three days (the book has been added to and retitled *Out of the Comfort Zone*).

By the grace of God, it became a best seller and paved the way for a book-writing ministry. He is faithful who promised.

SOUL SEARCH: Which of my works do I hesitate to commit fully to God?

⌒

**Father, I surrender all to you afresh today.
Amen.**

July 6

WHAT WE OWN

The LORD has made all for Himself,
yes, even the wicked for the day of doom.
—PROVERBS 16:4

The Bible asks the rhetorical question as to what we have that we didn't receive. The answer is that we have nothing. We don't own anything because everything belongs to God.

He created our eyes, our heart, the air we breathe, and the brain with which we think. He even owns our very souls, and they will go back to Him when we die.

He made all things for Himself. Everything was made for His pleasure. Think of all the animals, the colorful birds, and the beautiful flowers that we pick and give to others. All of it belongs to God.

For from Him, and to Him, and through Him are all things (Romans 11:36). That is such a consoling thought for those who love and trust Him.

SOUL SEARCH: How deep is my appreciation that almighty God made me and then proved His great love for me through the cross?

**Father, may I detest anything that seeks
to come between you and me. Amen.**

July 7

BITTER ENEMIES

Everyone proud in heart is an abomination to the LORD;
though they join forces, none will go unpunished.
—PROVERBS 16:5

*K*ing Herod and Pilate were bitter enemies, but they became friends in their antichrist spirit. This world may not agree on much, but they will gladly unify in spirit at the thought that God is too benevolent to have a judgment day, let alone create a literal hell.

Though they should clasp hands to join in agreement, they should know that it is easier to put out the sun with a garden hose than to stop God from having His day of justice. It will most certainly take place.

The wicked will be punished. Good will triumph over evil, and equity will have her way. We have the immutability of God's Word that it will happen, and there's nothing more sure than that.

SOUL SEARCH: Do I love justice and long for it, or is there some part of me that fears it?

Father, let me long to bring the equity of the cross
to a condemned, helpless, and hopeless world. Amen.

PERFECT RIGHTEOUSNESS

In mercy and truth atonement is provided for iniquity;
and by the fear of the LORD one departs from evil.
—PROVERBS 16:6

Mercy and truth were manifest at the cross. The mercy of the Father was expressed toward guilty sinners by the One who said He was the Truth. It was also at the bloody cross that righteousness and peace kissed each other. We can have peace with the perfect righteousness of God's law, because its wrath fell on Jesus and not on us. After seeing such love and wrath mingle in His precious blood, how can we not tremble in fear?

The fear of God is frowned upon by this sinful world, but it is the very foundation of a healthy walk with God. He who lacks the fear of the Lord lacks the motivation for departing from sin, and that will be to his eternal downfall.

SOUL SEARCH: What motivates me to keep my heart free of sin?

Father, today may I both love you
and tremble in fear of you. Amen.

PEACEFUL ENEMIES

When a man's ways please the LORD,
he makes even his enemies to be at peace with him.

—PROVERBS 16:7

The cross made a way for wicked sinners to please the Lord. The moment Jesus cried, "It is finished," the debt for sin was paid in full. The scales were balanced, and so our case could be dismissed.

We who were once enemies of God in our minds by wicked works could now be friends with God. But more than that, we could call Him "Father." He no longer stands over us in wrath as our Judge; He is now our Savior.

What a joy it is to know that we can please God. He rejoices over us with singing, and when we breathe our last, we can have full assurance that He will hold us in the palm of His faithful hand and preserve us for eternity—all because of the cross.

SOUL SEARCH: Which former enemy of mine is now at peace with me?

Father, I pray for the salvation of those who dislike me because I trust in you. Amen.

July 10

CHRIST, WHO IS OUR LIFE

Better is a little with righteousness,
than vast revenues without justice.
—PROVERBS 16:8

The gift of righteousness that we have in Christ is like the gift of a parachute, handed to a man just before he is about to jump out of a plane ten thousand feet in the air. Think of how terrifying and hopeless he would feel if he knew that he was going to have to jump without it. Then think of how he would feel as he held onto it with every ounce of his being. There is no way he is going to let it go, because it is his life.

The Bible says, "Put on the Lord Jesus Christ" (Romans 13:14), and calls Him, "Christ, who is our life" (Colossians 3:4). He is more than precious to us!

Be content with the little you have, and never let the temptation to love money corrupt you. And never, ever let sin distract you from the jump you will someday make.

SOUL SEARCH: Do I value the Savior as I should? How could I value Him more?

⁓

Father, you are my precious life. Amen.

MOUNTAIN TO A VALLEY

A man's heart plans his way,
but the LORD directs his steps.
—PROVERBS 16:9

We devise plans for the future, but life so often gets in the way. The Bible tells us not to boast of tomorrow, because we don't know what it will bring (Proverbs 27:1). Storms of tribulation can appear out of the blue and rain on our plans. Today I may be on a mountain, and tomorrow in a valley.

That's frightening, if life is random as many believe.

But the Christian believes that nothing is random. Nothing happens without the permissive will of God. He directs our steps because we acknowledge Him in all our ways. That is consoling. With trust in God in the equation, tomorrow is no longer dark. The path of the just is as a burning light that shines more and more each day. May you and I know the reality of that today.

SOUL SEARCH: What is one time when I clearly saw God directing my steps?

Father, I acknowledge you today as my Lord in every area of my life. Amen.

July 12

A DULL SPARK

Divination is on the lips of the king;
his mouth must not transgress in judgment.
—PROVERBS 16:10

*J*esus Christ is the King of kings. To compare any earthly king to Him is to compare a dull spark to the brightness of the sun at noon. He is a burning passion of holiness, with the divine sentence of wrath on His lips for wicked humanity.

The Scriptures warn that it's a fearful thing to fall into His holy hands. It will be a terror beyond words, because His mouth will not transgress in judgment. He will be justified on that day. No sinner will be able to lift his head and say, "God, you are wrong. I am innocent!"

Yet this same Judge caused the divine sentence to fall upon the sacrificial Lamb. God was manifest in the flesh and endured the wrath of the law upon Himself, so we could be forgiven and justified in Christ.

SOUL SEARCH: How is the Jesus in the pages of the Scriptures a living reality in my life?

∽

**Father, may you use me this day to say "a word in season"
to those who are weary (Isaiah 50:4).**

THE CHARACTER OF GOD

Honest weights and scales are the LORD's;
all the weights in the bag are His work.

—PROVERBS 16:11

We take our moral absolutes directly from the hand of God. With Him there are no variables, nor shadow of turning (James 1:17). It is offensive to the world when we say that with God things are either black and white. But they are.

He has written in His Law that it is always wrong to lie and steal, but it was wrong long before it was penned in stone. The moral law is the manifestation of the very character of God. A just weight has always been required, even before there were scales as we know them. This is because theft has always been morally wrong.

Therefore, we must be just in all of our dealings with others because it is the right thing to do.

SOUL SEARCH: In what ways am I trying to conform to the likeness of Jesus daily?

Father, may I show love to sinners and hatred for sin today. Amen.

A REPULSIVE THOUGHT

It is an abomination for kings to commit wickedness,
for a throne is established by righteousness.
—PROVERBS 16:12

*I*f it's an abomination for earthly kings to commit wickedness because a throne is established in righteousness, how much more so with God!

It's a repulsive thought indeed that our holy Creator would ever commit wickedness, and yet those who deem Him to be too loving and kind to punish sin are accusing Him of such. It would be wicked if God didn't judge murderers and rapists. It would be like an earthly (and evil) judge looking the other way when a violent crime was committed.

Of course there will be a judgment day, and of course there is a very real hell. God's righteousness calls for it, and His justice will be satisfied by it. May such thoughts help us to rid ourselves of the fears that so often hinder us from reaching out to the lost with the message of His mercy!

SOUL SEARCH: Do I consider all sins an abomination, or are there some that I look upon as less weighty?

**Father, cause me to be like the Savior,
loving righteousness and hating iniquity. Amen.**

July 15

NEW CREATURES

Righteous lips are the delight of kings,
and they love him who speaks what is right.

—PROVERBS 16:13

It's not in the human heart to delight in righteous lips. We naturally love evil speaking; the poison of asps is under our lips (Romans 3:13).

But when we come to the Savior, God changes our hearts. He makes us new creatures in Christ, loving righteousness and fighting the iniquity in our hearts. Now we, like Paul, delight in the law of God after the inward man, and we love those who speak the truth. Our hearts rejoice when godly men and women bravely stand for what is right, and especially when they uncompromisingly proclaim the gospel of light in this dark and sinful world.

SOUL SEARCH: Do I truly "delight in the law of God according to the inward man" (Romans 7:22)? How do I know this?

Father, search me and know my heart; "see if there is any wicked way in me" (Psalm 139:23–24). Amen.

GOOD NEWS FOR SINNERS

> As messengers of death is the king's wrath,
> but a wise man will appease it.
>
> —PROVERBS 16:14

The Bible calls death an enemy (1 Corinthians 15:26). That's good news for guilty sinners, because it means that death could be defeated.

It was because of sin that the death sentence justly hung over every son and daughter of Adam, like the dark and ominous shadow of a massive guillotine. But the wisdom of God sent light into the darkness and caused it to flee! The law that demanded our execution was pacified the moment the Son of God cried, "It is finished!" (John 19:30).

The debt had been paid. In the hymn "And Can It Be That I Should Gain?" Charles Wesley writes: "My chains fell off … I rose, went forth, and followed Thee."

SOUL SEARCH: If I wrote a song of redemption in my heart, what would the words be?

⌖

**Father, make my heart sing of your love today.
Amen.**

July 17

CLOUD OF MERCY

In the light of the king's face is life,
and his favor is like a cloud of the latter rain.

—PROVERBS 16:15

*M*oses spoke of the Lord lifting up the light of His countenance and shining peace upon Israel (Numbers 6:24–26). While God is just and holy, He takes no pleasure in the death of the wicked. His mercy triumphs over His justice. He would rather give humanity His smile than His frown.

The religious seek His favor, but they can never have peace with God while they are in their sins, and no amount of religious works will turn His face from justice.

However, in the glorious gospel we have a cloud of mercy waiting to rain upon the humble of heart. May God rain His Holy Spirit upon the lost, and may we be quick to run to them with the gospel of peace—of His favor in Christ.

SOUL SEARCH: Does my eternal salvation rest on grace alone, or do I feel I need to try to earn it?

≈⊘

**Father, thank you that I have everlasting life
because of your grace alone. Amen.**

July 18

WISDOM IS BETTER

How much better to get wisdom than gold!
And to get understanding is to be chosen rather than silver!
—PROVERBS 16:16

Gold is said to hold its value in a recession. Unlike most materials, it doesn't burn; rather, it is purified under heat. It improves when it's put in the fire. But the Scriptures tell us that wisdom is better. It never loses its value, and it tends to be more valued by the wise when they go through the fire.

When the Bible condemns "vain repetitions" (Matthew 6:7), it's in the context of chanting prayers, or repeating them over and over in mindless penance. Jesus encouraged importunity—persistence when it comes to prayer.

How we need wisdom as we face each day. So don't be afraid to seek God each day for wisdom. If you get wisdom from God and make the right decisions in life, it will save you much pain.

SOUL SEARCH: When was the last time I trusted in my own wisdom rather than God's?

⤳

**Father, may I have the wisdom to seek you
for wisdom today. Amen.**

HIGHWAY TO HEAVEN

The highway of the upright is to depart from evil;
he who keeps his way preserves his soul.

—PROVERBS 16:17

No one is on the highway to heaven without repentance from sin. Repentance takes place when we depart from evil. But it is grace that saves a sinner, and grace alone. The Scriptures couldn't be any more clear: "For by grace you have been saved through faith, and that not of yourselves; it is the gift of God, not of works, lest anyone should boast" (Ephesians 2:8–9).

Some say that all that is required of a sinner is to "believe," and that to say that repentance is necessary is to say that repentance is a "work." Then they should say the same thing about having to believe. The truth is, neither believing nor repenting saves us. Together, they are the highway that brings us to the grace of God for the preservation of the soul.

SOUL SEARCH: Has grace taught my heart to fear and also relieved my fears? Which have I experienced more readily?

Father, may grace be forever amazing for me.
Amen.

THE DEFIANT FIST

> Pride goes before destruction,
> and a haughty spirit before a fall.
> —PROVERBS 16:18

The letter *i* is right in the middle of the word *pride*, and the exaltation of self is at the core of the sin. From the moment we are born, we arrogantly think that the universe was made for us and that humanity is nothing but a servant for us and our will.

If godly parenting doesn't correct that assertion at an early age, another monster will enter society and bring in its train a trail of misery. Pride gives access to the darkest of demons and manifests itself in arrogance, ego, condescension, racism, and a thousand other secret sins.

Pride is the bastion of rebellion and holds its fist high in defiance of the will of the Creator. Those who serve it will fall into the hands of the living God, and eventually into eternal destruction. May we avoid pride like the plague.

SOUL SEARCH: Is God my copilot, or have I given Him the wheel?

Father, let me be free from self-exultation. Amen.

July 21

GETTING BETTER

Better to be of a humble spirit with the lowly,
than to divide the spoil with the proud.
—PROVERBS 16:19

"*B*etter" is only satisfied when best is achieved, and only God can claim to be the best at anything. Better is a carrot for which we should all strive. We always need to be better husbands, better wives, better neighbors, better students, better preachers, and better when it comes to reaching out to the lost.

The biggest better, however, is the better that says that we should be of a humble spirit with the lowly, because the door of eternal salvation has been set very low.

God resists the proud and gives grace to the humble, and grace is the door to heaven. Pride may promise pleasure, but it can't deliver eternal life to dying and damned sinners. Better we humble our hearts and end up in heaven than keep our arrogance and pride and end up in hell.

SOUL SEARCH: Who would I rather be with, the proud or those who have a humble attitude?

Father, may I show grace to the humble. Amen.

JOY AND PEACE IN BELIEVING

He who heeds the word wisely will find good,
and whoever trusts in the LORD, happy is he.
—PROVERBS 16:20

Happiness is rarely addressed in the Scriptures, possibly because human happiness is so dependent on what "happens" to us in life.

It is life's tragedies that so can easily steal our happiness in a moment of time. But they can never steal our joy. This is because joy isn't derived from what happens to us, but from whom we trust.

The apostle Paul spoke of having "joy and peace in believing" (Romans 15:13), and no one can take our joy and peace from us as long as we trust in Him who is faithful. Isaiah said that God will keep him in perfect peace, whose mind is stayed on Him (Isaiah 26:3).

Happiness (for which the world forever strives) is a crystal vase waiting to be shattered. However, the joy of the Lord is the strength of the godly (Nehemiah 8:10). So stay strong by having an unwavering trust in God.

SOUL SEARCH: Do I have a reputation for handling matters wisely, or do my decisions tend to stem from human "wisdom"?

**Father, help me to handle life with
godly wisdom. Amen.**

July 23

SOWING AND REAPING

The wise in heart will be called prudent,
and sweetness of the lips increases learning.

—PROVERBS 16:21

How fortunate we are when we realize that kindness, love, goodness, gentleness, and patience are virtues to be prized. Those who sow hatred, anger, selfishness, and greed will eventually reap bitterness and pain both on themselves and those around them. Nothing is sweet about such people or their relationships with those they profess to love.

But the godly have learned the great biblical truth that "whatever a man sows, that he will also reap" (Galatians 6:7). Sow kindness to others and you will reap kindness from others. Sow love to those around you and you will reap love from those around you. Those who do this are prudent, and they are truly wise in heart.

SOUL SEARCH: What are some of the ways I sow love to those around me?

⁓

**Father, help me to sow kindness in some
small way today. Amen.**

July 24

CREATED FOR GOD

Understanding is a wellspring of life to him who has it.
But the correction of fools is folly.

—PROVERBS 16:22

*H*ow terrible it is to live in the kingdom of darkness, having the understanding darkened and being alienated from the life of God. How our hearts should break for those who have no idea of their origins, the purpose for their existence, and where they will spend eternity.

As Christians, we understand that we were created by God and for God, and that we will spend eternity with Him enjoying pleasures forevermore. We also understand how sin destroys, why we need the Savior, why there is suffering, why there is so much evil, and how God can grant a dying sinner everlasting life in an instant.

His Word is a wellspring of life that instructs us in the things that matter most.

SOUL SEARCH: Do I truly believe that I will have "pleasures forevermore" (Psalm 16:11)? How is my faith evidenced by my joy?

⟿

**Father, let your joy always be my strength
(Nehemiah 8:10). Amen.**

THE REAL YOU

The heart of the wise teaches his mouth,
and adds learning to his lips.

—PROVERBS 16:23

Your heart is the real you. It's your soul, your very essence. What is your heart's deepest desire? Does your soul pant after God as David's did (Psalm 42:1)?

Do you yearn above all else to do His will? Then you will want to "preach the gospel to every creature" (Mark 16:15), for that was the reason for His suffering on the cross. He defeated death for dying sinners, and has commanded us to reach out to them with the message of everlasting life.

That is why the wise in heart teaches his mouth. He wants to add learning to his lips. He wants to be a workman who needs not be ashamed of the gospel (2 Timothy 2:15), and who has an answer for everyone who asks a reason for the hope that is in him (1 Peter 3:15).

SOUL SEARCH: What is my heart's deepest desire today?

**Father, may my life this day evidently glorify you.
Amen.**

July 26

HARSH WORDS

Pleasant words are like a honeycomb,
sweetness to the soul and health to the bones.

—PROVERBS 16:24

There are some godless people who don't believe in the existence of the human soul. But the soul is of the life, and every living body has a life. Without the soul, we are nothing but a dead body.

It's the godless who fail to realize the damage that can be done to the soul by harsh words. Many children have been scarred for life by being told that they are a loser or that they are not wanted. This often builds into a bitterness, anger, or even a hatred that results in what is commonly called psychosomatic illness.

But pleasant words are health to the bones. Many a young soul has been affirmed for life because a father or mother told them that they were dearly loved. Such pleasant words are as sweet as honey.

SOUL SEARCH: When was the last time I spoke harshly to someone? What would help me keep my words gentle?

**Father, may my words always be pleasing to you
(Psalm 19:14). Amen.**

July 27

THE COMPASS NEEDLE

There is a way that seems right to a man,
but its end is the way of death.

—PROVERBS 16:25

*T*his world is attracted to self-righteousness like a compass needle is attracted to the north. It "seems right" that God would require us to live good lives, and it "seems right" that if we do live good lives, we will make it to heaven.

I once had hernia surgery and was told that it would take about six weeks to recover. But after just one week, I felt fine. I was even running up stairs. This was because I was on pain medication—opiates—and they fooled me into a sense of wellness. When I stopped taking them, I found that I could hardly walk a few steps without excruciating pain.

Self-righteousness is an opiate that gives us a false sense of well-being before God. That's why we must use the moral law to bring the knowledge of sin, and show sinners their true state of spiritual health, painful though it may be.

SOUL SEARCH: Am I ever tempted to go a day without feeding on God's Word? What most often keeps me from my time with the Lord?

◞◟

Father, "oh, that my ways were directed to keep your statutes!" (Psalm 119:5). Amen.

BEAUTIFUL MANSIONS

The person who labors, labors for himself,
for his hungry mouth drives him on.
—PROVERBS 16:26

*I*magine spending your whole life laboring for yourself. What a tragic waste of precious time, because whatever you accomplish will become the property of others.

The world is full of beautiful mansions that were once owned by the rich, and they are now nothing more than cold museums because the rich person died and left this life empty-handed. His hungry mouth craved more, bigger, and better. And what did he end up with? Nothing.

Jesus spoke of a man like that. He wanted bigger barns for all of his worldly goods. He wasn't rich toward God, and that night death seized him (Luke 12:13–21). Labor instead for your Master. Crave His smile above all else. When we do that, we store up treasure in heaven.

SOUL SEARCH: What am I doing to seek God's smile today?

⤙◦⤚

**Father, "I will praise you with uprightness of heart,
when I learn your righteous judgments" (Psalm 119:7).
Amen.**

July 29

CLOSET SKELETONS

An ungodly man digs up evil,
and it is on his lips like a burning fire.
—PROVERBS 16:27

*E*ach of us has an army of dry-bone skeletons in the closet. What's more, a sinful world likes the closet door being open wide. Gossip sells like hot cakes on a cold day in Alaska.

How grateful I am that my closet is empty because of Calvary. The burning lips of gossip have nothing to say about the Christian who trusts alone in Jesus Christ, because our sins are washed away by His precious blood.

It isn't hard to dig up evil about any human being, because it doesn't sit very deep in the dirt. But all those things we are now ashamed of don't exist in the eyes or mind of God. Dig all they may, there is no treasure there.

SOUL SEARCH: Do I delight in digging up evil, or do I run the other way from gossip?

Father, I thank you that all my evil has been forgotten in Christ. Amen.

July 30

EVIL AGENDA

A perverse man sows strife,
and a whisperer separates the best of friends.
—PROVERBS 16:28

God forbid that we should sow or cultivate anything within the body of Christ that divides brethren and causes strife.

We know from the Scriptures that our battle is not against flesh and blood, but against a spiritual enemy (Ephesians 6:12) whose agenda is to kill, steal, and destroy (John 10:10). And we accommodate the enemy when we have fertile soil waiting for his poisonous seed.

Don't have a heart that is willing to listen to a whisperer. Harden the soil. Determine not to pay attention to gossip or potential slander. That sort of seed only produces bad fruit. It is heartbreaking when whisperers separate those who were once dear friends. The world does it all the time, but we can't let it happen within the body of Christ. The stakes are too high.

SOUL SEARCH: Am I a whisperer, or do I turn a deaf ear to such people?

**Father, make me a unifier of brethren.
Amen.**

LOVERS OF VIOLENCE

A violent man entices his neighbor,
and leads him in a way that is not good.

—PROVERBS 16:29

I will never forget the sight of the Los Angeles riots of 1992. Helicopter news footage recorded a man by the name of Reginald Denny stopping at a traffic light and then being dragged from his semi-trailer truck and severely beaten by a mob. I witnessed live footage of a concrete brick being thrown at his head, nearly killing him. Then I watched in horror as the man who threw the brick danced with joy after nearly killing an innocent man.

But it shouldn't have shocked me. In describing human nature, the Bible says, "Their feet are swift to shed blood" (Romans 3:15 NIV). We hardly think twice about how millions of people pack into movie theaters and sit in front of TV screens to be entertained by the spilling of human blood. The entertainment industry entices these millions, leading them in a way that is not good, and that is reflected in an ever increasingly violent society.

SOUL SEARCH: Am I a lover of violence, or does it horrify my heart?

**Father, help me to only love what you love.
Amen.**

August

August 1

THE ABUNDANCE
OF THE HEART

He winks his eyes to devise perverse things;
he purses his lips and brings about evil.

—PROVERBS 16:30

*E*vil always begins in the human heart. It is devised. The influence comes from within rather than without. This is a foundational biblical truth that the world refuses to accept—that man to the core is evil.

Jesus said that out of the heart comes evil things. He said that the mouth speaks "out of the abundance of the heart" (Luke 6:45). The reluctance to acknowledge blame is often seen when someone does something that is clearly evil, like the deliberate killing other human beings. Instead of speaking of the murderer as being evil, it's said that he struggled with mental problems, or that he came from a broken family. The culprit becomes the victim of mitigating circumstances, and the wickedness is justified rather than condemned.

This will not be the case on judgment day.

SOUL SEARCH: What do I need to change today so my heart will be pure?

**Father, help me today to guard my
heart from evil. Amen.**

BADGE OF HONOR

The silver-haired head is a crown of glory,
if it is found in the way of righteousness.

—PROVERBS 16:31

Gray hair speaks of experience. It's a badge of honor if our life is spent in service of God. Either we serve righteousness or we serve sin. God is our Master or we are slaves of the devil.

Gill's Bible commentary says, "Gray hairs, white locks through age are very ornamental; look very beautiful, bespeak gravity, wisdom, and prudence, and command reverence and respect; with the ancient Romans, greater honor was paid to age than to family or wealth; and the elder were revered by the younger next to God, and in the stead of parents; if it be found in the way of righteousness."*

Let's be forever found in the way of righteousness, and let's never allow sin to steal our crown.

SOUL SEARCH: What is my life spent in the service of? Is it God or something else?

⟳

Father, let me be your faithful servant. Amen.

---

* *John Gill's Exposition of the Bible* (Proverbs 16:31), Biblestudytools.com, http://www.biblestudytools.com/commentaries/gills-exposition-of-the -bible/proverbs-16-31.html.

EASY TARGET

He who is slow to anger is better than the mighty,
and he who rules his spirit than he who takes a city.

—PROVERBS 16:32

We are in a very real battle, and as part of the battle the Bible says that we must "rule" our spirit (see Romans 6:11–13). This is because the human spirit is naturally unruly. It bucks against the government of God. It is an unbroken stallion wanting to kick and fight against all that is holy.

Everything in the Christian life takes steadfast discipline. We buck against the thought of holiness, and against witnessing, fellowship, fasting, giving, prayer, and reading the Word of God. The world attracts us, the flesh tears us, and the devil tempts us. Without the indwelling Holy Spirit, we are nothing but helpless fish in a very small barrel. We are an easy target.

But if we rule our spirit in Christ, we are "more than conquerors through Him who [loves] us" (Romans 8:37).

SOUL SEARCH: Do I rule my appetites, or do they rule me?

∽

Father, help me to control all of my desires.
Amen.

NOT A FLEA JUMPS

The lot is cast into the lap,
but its every decision is from the Lord.
—PROVERBS 16:33

Not a flea jumps, nor a dog barks, nor a breath is drawn without the permission of almighty God. If He so decrees, the flea doesn't jump, the dog doesn't bark, and we don't draw another breath. If God sees fit to say, "Tonight your soul is required of you," our life as we know it is over.

This is comforting for the Christian, but not for the ungodly. It is offensive to him to think that if he rolls the dice, God can determine if he wins or loses. But whether he believes it or not, every hair on his head is numbered by the God who created him, and every mundane sparrow is seen by His omniscient eye.

SOUL SEARCH: Am I aware of God's presence at this very moment? How can I keep His presence in mind as I go about my day?

**Father, thank you that you are always present
and that you are the lover of my soul. Amen.**

DRY PRETZELS

Better is a dry morsel with quietness,
than an house full of feasting with strife.
—PROVERBS 17:1

*B*etter to eat dry and tasteless pretzels and have a smooth flight, than to feast on tender steak and gravy in severe turbulence.

Quietness isn't just the absence of sound. Someone may live in silence and yet be horribly disquieted within. Jesus had such peace in a fierce storm that He fell into a deep sleep. He had quietness within because His trust in His Father was impenetrable.

Have that same trust in your Father when you are in a storm. As long as you hold up your shield of faith (Ephesians 6:16), you will find that the "fiery darts" of the enemy cannot take away your quietness and peace.

SOUL SEARCH: When was the last time I dropped my shield of faith? What can I do to keep a better hold on it?

〰

**Father, help me to completely trust you today.
Amen.**

THE TWO SERVANTS

A wise servant will rule over a son who causes shame,
and will share an inheritance among the brethren.

—PROVERBS 17:2

*J*esus spoke of two servants. One wasn't wise. He said in his heart, "My master is delaying his coming" (Matthew 24:48) and began to play the hypocrite.

Just like that wicked servant, there are millions who secretly give themselves to sin. Their problem is, like the deceitful servant, they call Jesus "Lord." But He's not their Lord at all, and when He comes in wrath, they will think that they can continue with the playact and cry, "Lord, Lord." But Jesus will say that He never knew them (Matthew 7:21–23).

They are workers of lawlessness. They will have no inheritance among the brethren. What a horror beyond words, to be deceived by sin and to experience the ultimate rejection: "Depart from Me, all you workers of iniquity" (Luke 13:27).

SOUL SEARCH: Does the thought of hypocrisy in my own life horrify me? What hypocrisy do I tend to overlook?

**Father, help me to always be genuine
in my walk with you. Amen.**

UNBEARABLE HEAT

The refining pot is for silver,
and the furnace for gold,
but the LORD tests the hearts.

—PROVERBS 17:3

*T*he refining pot is the vessel that was used to heat up and purify silver. Life is full of refining pots for the Christian.

Maybe you're in a refining pot at the moment, and all you are feeling is the unbearable heat. You're so consumed by what you're going through that you can't see how the slightest good could come from it. Romans 8:28 seems empty and distant. All you can see is the teeth of lions.

But that's where faith comes in and shuts their mouths. We are told in Hebrews 11:33 that faith shut the lions' mouths, which is most likely a reference to Daniel in the lions' den. It's a hint that Daniel trusted that God had allowed such terror to purify him, and we know from the Scriptures that it did. So let's resolve to follow his godly example and let faith lift us above the lions today.

SOUL SEARCH: Is Romans 8:28 my great safety-net promise? What other verse(s) do I claim?

**Father, help me to always see your
hand in all things. Amen.**

UNFORTUNATE CIRCUMSTANCES

An evildoer gives heed to false lips;
a liar listens eagerly to a spiteful tongue.
—PROVERBS 17:4

Few people are called "wicked" by this world. The word, like the word *evil*, is reserved for mass murderers. But even then they talk about the person who committed the murders as having "mental" issues, so that his "evil" was shaped by unfortunate circumstances.

The Bible plays no such word games. It says that our heart—the very core of our being—is both wicked and deceitful (Jeremiah 17:9). As Christians we don't flinch at such words because we know they are true. We know our own hearts.

We also know that the world has a wrong definition of "good," and so it automatically has a wrong definition of "evil." When God says "good," He means moral perfection, and when He says "evil," He means anything that falls short of that perfect moral standard. That changes everything, for those who care to think about it.

SOUL SEARCH: How do I think of myself? Do I consider myself a basically good person?

∽

**Father, teach me to discern between
good and evil. Amen.**

THE POOR
HEARD GLADLY

He who mocks the poor reproaches his Maker;
he who is glad at calamity will not go unpunished.

—PROVERBS 17:5

The Bible says that God makes the rich and the poor (Proverbs 22:2). That flies in the face of many prosperity preachers who say that it's God's will for all Christians to be rich. But that's not true experientially, biblically, or historically.

The foundational teaching of the prosperity movement is that being poor is a curse. It is true that it's not good to be unable to pay bills or put food on the table for your family. But at the same time, we are told that riches can be a curse (Proverbs 30:8–9), and "the love of money is a root of all kinds of evil," causing some to stray from the faith (1 Timothy 6:10).

We are also told that the poor gladly heard Jesus. Like the beggar named Lazarus (see Luke 16:19–31), the poor will enter heaven because their lack of riches caused them to look to God for His mercy in Christ. On that day they will be rich indeed.

SOUL SEARCH: Do I envy the unsaved rich or do I pity them? Why?

⌁

Father, may I esteem the riches that matter.
Amen.

THE FAMILY UNIT

Children's children are the crown of old men,
and the glory of children is their father.

—PROVERBS 17:6

*I*n recent years we have seen a dissipation of the family unit. Not only do people shack up together, but mothers are left to raise their children without the stabilization of fathers. The fathers have shirked their responsibility to raise their own offspring, and this has had a devastating effect on society.

Fathers are not the glory of children, because the children don't even know who the fathers are. So we have kids who grow up with no respect for the police and law, and, more importantly, no fear of God. They lie, steal, and kill, and couldn't care less.

Psalm 11:3 asks, "If the foundations are destroyed, what can the righteous do?" The only answer is for us to preach the everlasting foundation of the gospel as we've never done before.

SOUL SEARCH: Where do I find my stability? Is it in the knowledge of my Father's love?

**Father, help me to be content with the love
you expressed at the cross. Amen.**

August 11

WHAT IS EXCELLENT?

Excellent speech is not becoming to a fool,
much less lying lips to a prince.
—PROVERBS 17:7

What comes to mind when you think of "excellent speech"? Is it the words of the eloquent Dr. Martin Luther King Jr., or perhaps the brilliant William Shakespeare? Or is it the most compelling part of a movie or television program?

Every excellent word spoken fades into obscurity compared to the excellent speech that came from the eloquent lips of the Son of God. The Bible tells us that His hearers were amazed at His stirring words, even when He was a child.

But for millions, excellent speech is exemplified in the Sermon on the Mount. Some simple people say that Jesus of Nazareth never existed. If that is the case, tell us who spoke the amazing and unique words in that greatest of all sermons, and we will without hesitation fall at His feet and worship Him.

SOUL SEARCH: Who is my favorite speaker? Why?

Father, make me like the psalmist, who rejoiced at your words like someone who had found great treasure. Amen.

TURNING HEADS

A PRESENT IS A PRECIOUS STONE IN THE EYES OF ITS
POSSESSOR;
WHEREVER HE TURNS, HE PROSPERS. —PROVERBS 17:8

Bribery easily turns the head of those who are given to the love of money. Judas hung himself for the love of money, but had he seen the future he may not have been dazzled by silver.

Then there are millions of religious people who would probably say that they would never be given to bribery, yet they are unwittingly guilty of the crime. They believe that the way into heaven is to be a good person who believes in God and tries to do good things for others. They believe that their good works are pleasing to God, to a point where they will tip the scales of eternal justice.

They wrongly believe that because of their works, they will find entrance into heaven. What they fail to understand is that God's law leaves us as criminals before the ultimate Judge of the universe, who will not be bribed into turning His head and compromising eternal justice.

The only thing that can ever save a guilty sinner from the just damnation of hell is the mercy of the Judge—and He is rich in mercy.

SOUL SEARCH: Has my head ever been turned by a bribe? Is there any bribe that I'd agree to today?

∽

Father, let the thought of the slightest compromising of integrity be abominable to me. Amen.

MORAL FAILURES

He who covers a transgression seeks love,
but he who repeats a matter separates friends.
—PROVERBS 17:9

How we react to gossip, or even legitimate truths about someone's moral failure, is a barometer of the depth of our love. Are we as quick to cover another's shame as we would cover our own? Or do we, like a pack of hungry wolves, tear at the flesh to find a juicy morsel? Do we relish the taste, or do we refuse it as poison?

God, in Christ, covered our shameful transgressions using His life's blood, such was His love. That's the thought that should make distasteful what this world sees as delicious.

God only knows how many friendships have been destroyed, families broken apart, and churches split because we exposed rather than covered a transgression.

SOUL SEARCH: Do people consider me to be loving and kind? If not, what do I need to change?

*Father, give me an opportunity to express love
and kindness today. Amen.*

MAKING DUMB WISE

Rebuke is more effective for a wise man
than a hundred blows on a fool.
—PROVERBS 17:10

*S*cripture can make the dumbest of us wise. All it takes on our part is a listening ear that will send truth to the heart. But even legitimate rebuke is often hard for our proud Adamic nature to take to heart. We want to run from it rather than embrace it.

Many years ago a Christian friend noticed a flaw in my character (one of many). He saw that as a new Christian I would sometimes inject humor at an inappropriate moment. He gently took me aside and shared how the Scriptures say that to do so is like a filthy fly in a beautiful ointment.

That incident happened over forty years ago, but thankfully I have never forgotten what was said. It left a deep impression on me because it was based on Holy Scripture. His wise words have guided me in personal relationships and when witnessing to the lost, as well as in many pulpits.

SOUL SEARCH: Am I hurt by legitimate rebuke, or do I welcome it?

Father, please help me to always be
open to correction. Amen.

GIVEN TO JEALOUSY

An evil man seeks only rebellion;
therefore a cruel messenger will be sent against him.
—PROVERBS 17:11

This verse always reminds me of King Saul, and at the same time it makes me tremble. Saul gave himself to jealousy, and it wasn't long before that festered into hatred and then murder. That's what we see happen in the natural realm, but there is also a spiritual explanation.

Saul gave himself to rebellion, and in doing so opened himself to the demonic realm. A cruel messenger was sent against him. That word *against* in the original Hebrew language has reference to a pulling downward. Demons tormented the king and pulled him down.

This rebellious generation has given themselves to rebellion. They have embraced blasphemy, homosexuality, fornication, pornography, adultery, hatred, bitterness, and violence. They have opened themselves to cruel demons that will torment them in this life and drag them to hell in the next. May God have mercy on them, and may we reach out to them with the gospel and show them His mercy.

SOUL SEARCH: How do I feel when another person succeeds? Do I rejoice with them, or do I struggle with envy?

Father, please help me avoid evil and rebellion as I lean on you and draw on your wisdom. Amen.

BUILDING BIGGER BARNS

Let a man meet a bear robbed of her cubs,
rather than a fool in his folly.

—PROVERBS 17:12

*T*he Bible calls many people fools. A fool says in his heart that there is no God (Psalm 14:1). A fool builds big barns and isn't rich toward God (Luke 12:18). A fool makes a mock at sin (Proverbs 14:9), and a fool has no fear of God before his eyes (Romans 3:18). Because of that, you don't want to mess with him. A bear robbed of her offspring is pretty scary. She will rip you to pieces, so what does this verse mean?

A person who has no fear of God will lie to you, steal from you, and even murder you if he thinks he can get away with it. The common denominator in every murder case in history has been a lack of the fear of God. Those who fear God won't so much as hate someone, because they know that God equates hatred with murder, and that they'll have to face Him on judgment day.

Such sobering knowledge helps sin-loving sinners flee to the Savior and keep their hearts free of sin.

SOUL SEARCH: Do I always fear God? If not, how can I make it my resolution?

**Father, may I have a revelation today
as to what it means to fear you. Amen.**

August 17

THE JUDGMENTS OF GOD

> Whoever rewards evil for good,
> evil will not depart from his house.
>
> —PROVERBS 17:13

Skeptics and atheists often accuse God of being vindictive. They don't believe He exists, but they accuse Him of committing all sorts of atrocities, including killing men, women, and children in a worldwide flood that they don't believe happened.

While we have little idea of when and how God sends His judgments on the earth, we do know that if someone rewards evil for good, evil won't depart from his house. It would be interesting to do a study of the house and lineage of Judas Iscariot, after he rewarded the ultimate good with evil.

While God does take vengeance on all those who are evil, and while He does sometimes judge humanity, skeptics never dare say, "All of His judgments are righteous and true altogether." But they are.

SOUL SEARCH: Do I ever wish for judgment day for others, with no mercy? If so, why?

Father, I pray for the millions of unsaved human beings who don't know you. Amen.

GOLDEN ADVICE

The beginning of strife is like releasing water;
therefore stop contention before a quarrel starts.

—PROVERBS 17:14

*T*his godly advice is golden advice. It should be treasured. If we are wise, we will avoid contention like the plague.

If we must confront someone, it makes sense to ask a question rather than to be accusatory. To accuse with, "You said this!" will begin strife, while the question, "Did you say this?" is more likely to end in peace, not war. Churches have split, families have been horribly divided, and lifelong friendships have been destroyed because of unwise and contentious meddling.

Like water, contention has a life of its own. It's almost impossible to stop. So don't add to it. Leave it alone. If possible, just commit the problem to prayer and let the water dry up. Otherwise you will be overwhelmed with a flood that will take away almost everything in its path, leaving you devastated and wondering what happened.

SOUL SEARCH: When was the last time I was tempted to meddle? What was the result?

**Father, help me to be concerned only
with legitimate matters. Amen.**

CALLING EVIL GOOD

He who justifies the wicked, and he who condemns the just,
both of them alike are an abomination to the LORD.

—PROVERBS 17:15

This evil world will always protect its own by justifying the wicked. They justify the killing of children in the womb by saying it's a woman's choice, the sin of homosexuality by saying that the people were born that way, or the act of adultery by saying the marriage was bad.

Yet these things are morally wrong in God's eyes. We cannot and dare not call evil good and good evil just because the world tells us to. We instead warn them that God is uncompromisingly just and holy, and that there is coming a day when they will face pure holiness.

At the same time as they justify the wicked, the world condemns the just. They say that we are hateful, when love is our motivation for sounding the alarm. But our consolation in these things is that evil will eventually bow down to good. Justice will, in the end, prevail and triumph over injustice; those who love God will be vindicated; and He will be glorified.

SOUL SEARCH: When was the last time I was wrongly accused? Was I able to rejoice even amid that?

Father, help me to rejoice, be exceedingly glad,
and leap for joy when I'm persecuted for the
name of Jesus (Luke 6:23). Amen.

CHANGED PRIORITIES

Why is there in the hand of a fool the purchase
price of wisdom, since he has no heart for it?
—PROVERBS 17:16

How our priorities changed when we came to the Savior! When we were in the world, nothing else mattered but our personal happiness. God was not in our thoughts, but rather was a distant reality. We had no love for righteousness and saw no need for holiness. We were unthankful to God for the gift of life and completely self-centered. We had no heart for wisdom.

But the new birth brought a radical change. God translated us out of darkness into light (Colossians 1:13). He opened the eyes of our understanding and caused us to hunger and thirst after righteousness. Wisdom became our guide. We learned that righteousness must always take priority over our own personal happiness.

Now, we always want to do what is right in God's eyes. We want what God wants, saying, "Your will be done" (Matthew 6:10). That's wisdom.

SOUL SEARCH: Do I highly esteem wisdom? Why should I want to make it more of a priority in my life?

Father, make me wise in my thoughts and words.
Amen.

REAL FRIENDS

A friend loves at all times,
and a brother is born for adversity.

—PROVERBS 17:17

*T*here are some shallow people who say that a friend in need is a real pain. The original maxim is, "A friend in need is a friend indeed." That means that a friend (when you're in need) is a friend indeed. The idea is that fakes will flake, and true friends will show themselves as friends in times of adversity. This is because "a friend loves at all times" (Proverbs 17:17). A friend will give us a listening ear, an uplifting hand, and an encouraging word, and will gladly help us financially if we need it.

As Christians, our friendships shouldn't be confined to other Christians. Jesus was accused of being "a friend of … sinners" (Matthew 11:19). The task for us as Christians is to also be a friend of sinners.

We should let that thought challenge us. How many friends do we have in the world to whom we are reaching out with the gospel?

SOUL SEARCH: Is my love limited to Christians, or am I friends with non-Christians as well? What does my percentage of Christian versus non-Christian friends say about me?

∽

**Father, help me to let my light shine where it
will be seen. Amen.**

PROUD CREATURES

A man devoid of understanding shakes hands in a pledge,
and becomes surety for his friend.

—PROVERBS 17:18

*E*ven the most humble of us are proud creatures. Some may deny it, but most live for the praise of others. We want to impress our peers with our house, our car, or our clothes. It's not just the gold medal or the Oscar that we seek. It's what comes with it—the adulation, the applause, and the attention of the media. We love the show of appreciation, the roar of the crowd, the clicking cameras, and the admiring looks.

He is void of understanding indeed who, for the praise of others, vouches for a friend, to make them think he's a man of wealth when he's not. After the friends leave, he's left with a financial burden he didn't need.

The best way to defuse the desire for the praise of others is to instead seek the praise of God. Nothing impresses Him but a humble faith and a contrite spirit. Those who seek such will keep themselves from foolishness and save themselves a lot of pain.

SOUL SEARCH: Do I seek the praise of men, or do I care only for the praise of God?

✏

Father, may I seek only your praise. Amen.

August 23

LOVING TRANSGRESSION

He who loves transgression loves strife,
and he who exalts his gate seeks destruction.

—PROVERBS 17:19

There are many who love transgression. They love theft, lying, blasphemy, adultery, and even murder. The Bible speaks of men being not just perpetrators, but lovers of violence.

I remember in my youth loving theft. My friends and I had maps of orchards around our neighborhood, and we took great delight in stealing fruit, taking it back to our treehouse, and eating it in secret.

Yet our homes had no shortage of fruit. Theft tastes sweet to an evil heart. "Boys will be boys," some may say, but boys who steal often become men who steal, and hell is waiting for thieves (1 Corinthians 6:10). Evildoers seek their own will rather than God's will, and that will be to their eternal destruction.

May we never love transgression or strife or seek to justify it. May we instead be peacemakers, and in so doing prove ourselves to be children of the living God.

SOUL SEARCH: How do I feel about past sins? Do I ever get pleasure from the memory of them?

Father, help me to, like Jesus, hate iniquity.
Amen.

DEAF TO ITS VOICE

He who has a deceitful heart finds no good,
and he who has a perverse tongue falls into evil.

—PROVERBS 17:20

Those who love God must reckon their sinful heart dead in Christ. For the Christian, the Adamic nature was crucified on the cross with the Savior. We therefore no longer hear its voice. We know that it not only brought us no good, but, if left to itself, it would have also taken us to hell. It was a sinful heart that wanted to gossip, sow discord, boast of itself, and cause strife. It lived for itself and cared nothing for God.

Perverse tongues go with a deceitful heart and fall into evil. Matthew Henry said, "He that has a perverse tongue, spiteful and abusive, scurrilous or backbiting, falls into one mischief or other, loses his friends, provokes his enemies, and pulls trouble upon his own head. Many a one has paid dearly for an unbridled tongue."

SOUL SEARCH: How accurate would it be to say that my tongue is linked to my conscience? Why?

∽

Father, set at my mouth an armed guard to shoot down any gossip before it passes my lips. Amen.

---

* *Matthew Henry, An Exposition of the Old and New Testament* (London: Joseph Robinson Jr., 1839), 890.

POLITICAL CORRECTNESS

He who begets a scoffer does so to his sorrow,
and the father of a fool has no joy.

—PROVERBS 17:21

*T*he Bible isn't politically correct. Neither was Jesus. He called people fools, hypocrites, serpents, and foxes. You can always trust Him to speak the truth. And if we ignore His offer of everlasting life, we are fools in the truest sense of the word.

This verse is a reminder that every one of us has the individual freedom to make choices in this life. A man may have been brought up in the way of righteousness by godly parents, but in a moment of temptation he played the fool and committed adultery. Suddenly he loses his wife and kids. Sin has fearful repercussions in this life and in the next, and oftentimes one of those terrible consequences is to bring shame to the good family name and sorrow to those who bore him.

SOUL SEARCH: Do I contemplate the end results of sin, or do I tend to make snap decisions?

Father, open my eyes to the suffering that sin ushered in. Amen.

HOW TO MAKE MERRY

A merry heart does good, like medicine,
but a broken spirit dries the bones.

—PROVERBS 17:22

A merry heart is beneficial to our health. It does us good as does medicine, and if any human being should have a heart full of merriment, it's those who are trusting in Jesus Christ. We not only know God, but He has also translated us from the kingdom of darkness to the kingdom of light (Colossians 1:13), opened our understanding, forgiven our many sins, granted us everlasting life, promised never to leave us or forsake us, and told us that He will work everything that life throws at us to our good (Romans 8:28).

It is by trusting His promises that every mountain is made smooth, every valley filled, and every giant made into a helpless grasshopper. The fruit of faith in God is joy (Galatians 5:22). It's the barometer of the depth of faith we have in Him. So prove your trust by your joy, and "the joy of the LORD" will be your strength in the tough times (Nehemiah 8:10).

SOUL SEARCH: Do I have a merry heart all the time or just when life is going my way?

**Father, may you always be the center of
my greatest joy. Amen.**

August 27

LAWMAKERS

A wicked man accepts a bribe behind the back
to pervert the ways of justice.

—PROVERBS 17:23

*I*t is a sense of justice that most sets humans apart from the beasts. Every known civilization, no matter how seemingly primitive, has set up court systems and deals out justice for lawbreakers. This is because man is made in the image of God. Dogs, cats, horses, and cows don't set up judges and punish their kind for transgression of some law.

For this reason, humanity is without excuse when it comes to the reality of sin. Our God-given conscience is our personal barometer of right and wrong, and if it's doing its duty, it should lead us to the foot of the cross for mercy. No one can plead innocent on judgment day. On that day, perfect justice will be done. No one will be bribing the judge with "good" works, and no one will pervert the ways of judgment.

SOUL SEARCH: How primed is my conscience today?

**Father, let me always have a good conscience
before you. Amen.**

LIFE AND LIBERTY

Wisdom is in the sight of him who has understanding,
but the eyes of a fool are on the ends of the earth.

—PROVERBS 17:24

What could be a better summary of the human existence than the famous and esteemed "life, liberty,
and the pursuit of happiness"? "The pursuit of happiness" is
arguably the most famous phrase in the Declaration of Inde-
pendence, attributed by popular opinion to Thomas Jefferson.

However, such a philosophy has perhaps made fools of millions. This is because they set their eyes on the ends of the
earth to chase happiness—at any cost. Wisdom would rather
esteem life, appreciate liberty, and, above all other things, pursue "righteousness."

But as Christians, we are not as this world, which chooses
whatever draws it to happiness. We instead always choose what
is right, above that which makes us happy. It is righteousness
that tends to life, and righteousness that will deliver sinners
from wrath on the day of judgment.

SOUL SEARCH: When has my personal happiness taken
precedence over righteousness?

*Father, make me love righteousness and
always give it preeminence. Amen.*

THE PRODIGAL

A foolish son is a grief to his father,
and bitterness to her who bore him.

—PROVERBS 17:25

The parable of the prodigal son doesn't mention the boy's mother. When he went to a far country and spent all his money on prostitutes, we are not told that it was to the bitterness of his mother or that he even had a living mother. But we do know that his father was in grief, waiting for him to come to his senses and return home.

The grief of the father was turned to joy in a moment of time, when he saw his son a great way off returning to his home. His father ran to him, fell upon his neck, kissed him, and rejoiced that his son, who was dead, was now alive. The mother isn't mentioned because the emphasis of the story is on our heavenly Father, who rejoices when a sinner gets up out of the pigsty of his sins and comes to Him with a repentant heart.

We were dead in our sins, but were suddenly made alive in Christ. Such a sight brings joy to heaven itself.

SOUL SEARCH: When in my life have I been a prodigal?

**Father, thank you for bringing me to
my senses about my sin. Amen.**

STRUCK BY HEAVEN

Also, to punish the righteous is not good,
nor to strike princes for their uprightness.

—PROVERBS 17:26

According to the Scriptures, the crucifixion of the Son of God was the punishment of "the just for the unjust" (1 Peter 3:18). "For [God] made Him who knew no sin to be sin for us, that we might be the righteousness of God in Him" (2 Corinthians 5:21). The Prince of Peace was struck by heaven itself so that we could have equity.

The cross was not good. It was evil, terrible, and horrific that wicked sinners would take the perfect, sinless Lamb of God and cruelly crucify Him. Yet God was in Christ reconciling the world to Himself. We broke God's law and Jesus paid our fine.

It was not good, yet it was wonderful, glorious, and unspeakably magnificent, because in that cruel cross we see the love of God expressed to sinners such as us.

SOUL SEARCH: What does it mean for me to glory in the cross?

Father, deepen my understanding of the blood
of the cross and your love for me. Amen.

SPARED WORDS

He who has knowledge spares his words,
and a man of understanding is of a calm spirit.

—PROVERBS 17:27

We must spare our words, with the aim of being precise, when sharing the gospel with this world. It's been said that a good teacher can make profound truths simple so the simple can appreciate those profound truths.

It is a tragedy indeed that most of this world knows that Jesus Christ died for the sin of the world, but they don't understand the depth of the gospel—that His death was substitutionary. It is simple indeed that we can be saved from hell through childlike trust.

We have instead made the simple story complex and have left millions in darkness. The way to spare our words is to base the message on the Scriptures. Then, with the help of the Holy Spirit, we must faithfully produce an understanding that they are in terrible and eternal danger, and that they desperately need the Savior.

SOUL SEARCH: How have I grown in my understanding over my years as a Christian?

**Bread of heaven, feed me now
and ever more. Amen.**

September

WISE FOOLS

Even a fool is counted wise when he holds his peace;
when he shuts his lips, he is considered perceptive.

—PROVERBS 17:28

The problem is that a fool hasn't the wisdom to hold his peace, and most who are fools are too foolish to recognize that they're fools. This is why all of us should be swift to hear and slow to speak (James 1:19). We are fools compared to the wisdom of God.

The Bible tells us that the wisdom of this world is foolishness with God (1 Corinthians 3:19). Think of how many believe that we are talking primates, created by a causeless Big Bang in space, and how those who teach this foolishness are esteemed wise by this world. We are indeed a foolish race.

But when we're born again, we receive the mind of Christ. We need no longer be fools, as we sit at the feet of Jesus and learn from Him.

SOUL SEARCH: Could I be considered a discreet person? If so, why?

∽

Father, please teach me the art of discretion.
Amen.

NOT A GOOD GUIDE

A man who isolates himself seeks his own desire;
he rages against all wise judgment.

—PROVERBS 18:1

Natural desire is not a good guide; it will lead us away from God. That's because human desire was corrupted in Adam. We desire our own way from the womb, thinking that the world was made for us and other people were created to be our servants. In time, life teaches us otherwise. We eventually have to feed, clothe, and house ourselves. This sinful desire still insists on its own way, and if it can't get it, we will separate from others and refuse to listen to reason rather than yield to the desire of others.

But when we come to the cross, the sinful nature is crucified with Christ, and we then reckon all sinful desires dead (Romans 6:6–7). Now we have the wisdom from above, a wisdom that is peaceable and open to reason from others (James 3:17).

SOUL SEARCH: How can I reckon Adam dead in my life today?

**Father, may I this day walk in the newness of the life
I have in Christ. Amen.**

HEDONISM

A fool has no delight in understanding,
but in expressing his own heart.
—PROVERBS 18:2

Hedonism is "the pursuit of pleasure; sensual self-indulgence."* It would be safe to say that this is the priority of most of this world. Nothing matters to them but their own pleasure.

Now, that in itself isn't sinful; it's natural to want to be happy in life. However, if the virtue of understanding is discarded, then happiness alone is the pursuit of the fool.

If we study the parable of the sower, we will see that the good-soil hearer (the genuine convert) understood what he was hearing. Without an understanding of our sin and of the work of the cross, there can be no salvation. This is because the way to be saved is to "call upon the name of the Lord" (Acts 19:13), and no one will call upon Him to be saved if they don't understand that they need to be saved.

SOUL SEARCH: How well do I understand God's perspective on sin?

**Father, help me see my sin from your perspective,
and keep trusting in the Savior. Amen.**

---

* Oxford Dictionaries, s.v. "hedonism," https://en.oxforddictionaries.com/definition/hedonism.

MILITANT SINNERS

When the wicked comes, contempt comes also;
and with dishonor comes reproach.

—PROVERBS 18:3

*T*he more a man is given to darkness, the more he will hate the light. The more he gives himself to evil, the more he will despise and treat with contempt those who stand for the good.

We are mocked and hated because we say that marriage should be between a man and a woman, that we should be virgins until marriage, and that all life must be valued, both the child in the womb and the life of the elderly. Notice that Scripture says that the wicked are not passive. They are militant. They "come" and they bring utter contempt. They have an agenda of lawlessness, of shameful practices.

But we know that even if the whole world is given to evil, love must warn them that judgment day is coming, and that hell is the terrifying and just deserts of all who die in their sins.

SOUL SEARCH: Do I truly love the wicked? If so, how does my life show that?

✍

**Father, please help me to love the wicked enough
to warn them about the reality of hell. Amen.**

September 5

DEEP WATERS

The words of a man's mouth are deep waters;
the wellspring of wisdom is a flowing brook.

—PROVERBS 18:4

*D*eep waters can be terribly dangerous. They can contain hidden and deadly currents that can pull under the unwitting swimmer. However, a flowing brook contains no hidden surprises. It is fresh and transparent.

So take care where you get your advice. This world is more than willing to tell you what you should and shouldn't do. But it has a wisdom that is demonic, and one that fights against the biblical revelation of God. The words of the ungodly may seem right, but they can pull you under and take you to the depths of hell.

The Bible says that we are blessed if we don't listen to the counsel of the ungodly (Psalm 1:1). However, counsel that is based on the flowing brook of God's precious Word is full of life and truth, is for our eternal benefit, and is God-glorifying.

SOUL SEARCH: Who do I go to for advice about marriage, family, business, or forgiveness? Would their counsel be considered "godly"?

**Father, may you be the only source
of my wisdom. Amen.**

RESPECTER OF PERSONS

It is not good to show partiality to the wicked,
or to overthrow the righteous in judgment.

—PROVERBS 18:5

We're often impressed with looks, cool clothes, sports, wealth, and musical and acting talent. We respect persons.

But the Bible says that God is no respecter of persons (Acts 10:34). He isn't the slightest bit impressed with gold medals, sports prowess, money in the bank, or posh three-piece suits. This is because He looks upon the heart. He sees the thought life and the motive of every person who ever lived, and of every deed we've ever done.

It's grievous when the wicked are acquitted in a court of law—when justice is perverted because of celebrity bias or the sparkle of a rich person's diamonds. And it's even more grievous when the wicked overthrow the righteous in judgment. When that happens, it makes the godly whisper, "Come quickly, Lord Jesus."

SOUL SEARCH: How impressed am I with appearances?

**Father, help me to see everything
from your perspective. Amen.**

GOD-GIVEN SAFEGUARDS

A fool's lips enter into contention,
and his mouth calls for blows.
—PROVERBS 18:6

There are three God-given safeguards through which our words should pass before they make it into other people's ears. They should first pass the virtue of restraint before they pass our teeth and our lips.

But that's not enough for a fool. Restraint is ignored, and the teeth and lips are open wide so his foolish words enter into contention. Instead of putting out fire, he adds more fuel and gets himself burned.

If you ever detect contention in the air, be sure you exercise that godly virtue of restraint. Be meek, as was the Savior. Keep your tongue behind clenched teeth and within tight lips. If you are forced to speak, let it be with soft words that turn away wrath. In doing so, you will prove yourself to be wise—and save yourself some pain.

SOUL SEARCH: How important is my opinion to me?

**Father, help me to learn the virtue of restraint.
Amen.**

THE LIFE OF THE BODY

A fool's mouth is his destruction,
and his lips are the snare of his soul.

—PROVERBS 18:7

The Bible says that the human soul is the life of the body (Genesis 2:7). When the soul leaves the body, the body is left lifeless. This is why every soul-denying atheist will get the shock of his life (and death), when at death his soul departs from his body and passes on into eternity.

Jesus told us that our mouth speaks the abundance of the heart or the soul (Matthew 15:8). If our heart is full of sin, our lips will in time reveal it. He also said, "For by your words you will be justified, and by your words you will be condemned" (Matthew 12:37 KJV). If his lips pour out filth, lies, hatred, bitterness, and blasphemy, he will have his soul snared by the devil, and the devil will take him captive to further do his will.

So "keep your heart with all diligence," because from out of it are the "issues of life" (Proverbs 4:23).

SOUL SEARCH: What steps have I taken to obey the admonition to guard my heart with all diligence?

*Father, help me to guard what I let into my eyes,
ears, and my mind. Amen.*

THE GREATEST STORY

The words of a talebearer are as wounds,
and they go down into the innermost parts of the belly.
—PROVERBS 18:8 AKJV

Most of us carry some sort of wounds. Perhaps someone has said something that was cutting, and it caused us great pain. It wasn't a superficial wound that healed quickly. It went right down to the innermost parts of our very soul.

It's at the foot of the cross that we let go of past pain. We give the pain, the anger, the bitterness, the unforgiveness—all of it—to God, and then we forgive and forget. We leave behind all that the world laid upon us, and begin doing what we've been saved to do: seek and save those who are lost. We now become a carrier of the greatest story ever told—the gospel of everlasting life.

The words of a talebearer bring wounds. But as Christians we speak words that bring healing to a dying world.

SOUL SEARCH: When was the last time I used my words to bring healing?

**Father, teach me to bring healing words to those
that need them. Amen.**

PICK UP THE PIECES

He who is slothful in his work is a brother
to him who is a great destroyer.

—PROVERBS 18:9

*I*t's interesting to note that when Jesus fed the five thousand, He told His disciples to pick up the leftover bread. As Christians we should follow in His steps and take care not to waste our food, knowing it's a provision from God and that many go hungry on a daily basis.

Neither should we waste our money. Rather, we should use it first to take care of our family and then use it to further the kingdom of God.

We should also be careful not to waste our time. It is a wise man or woman who cries with the psalmist, "Teach us to number our days, that we might gain a heart of wisdom" (Psalm 90:12). We can waste our life by living for our own fleeting pleasures. Instead, we should use precious time to bring pleasure to heaven by seeking to save those who are lost.

SOUL SEARCH: How do I use my time? Do I value every minute of every day?

Father, please remind me to be wise with
my precious time. Amen.

BIG NAMES

The name of the LORD is a strong tower;
the righteous run to it and are safe.

—PROVERBS 18:10

*I*f you know someone with a big name, and they trust you enough to lend their name to you, it can open huge doors. That's why authors have a foreword written by a famous person, and why movie studios quote well-known reviewers on their promotional material. Certain names command respect in certain circles.

God entrusts His name to those who belong to the Savior, and He's given Jesus a name that is above every name. Those who have despised His wonderful name and used it to cuss will bow the knee to Him. What a day of terror that will be for them.

But for those who have been made righteous by the grace of God in Christ, it will be a day of unspeakable joy. It will be the ultimate honor to bow the knee to the name that causes demons to tremble and bids the flight of angels.

SOUL SEARCH: Do I tend to name drop, or do I take advantage of the power God has given me through prayer?

**Father, thank you for giving me the name
of Jesus in which to pray. Amen.**

September 12

THE REPLACER
OF FAITH

The rich man's wealth is his strong city,
and like a high wall is his own esteem.

—PROVERBS 18:11

The love of money is a subtlety that can silently replace faith in God. We can trust in money rather than in God, and so money can become our source of peace, the supplier of our needs, and our source of joy.

A poor man can have a covetous heart despite his poverty, and a rich man can have wealth but his wealth may not be his first love. It isn't his idol or his strong city, because God is his only refuge. His God is the supplier of his needs, his great source of peace and joy, and his high wall of protection from the future.

The key is for each of us to have a loose hand with our money. We should give regularly to our church, to faithful ministries, to the poor, and to every good and godly cause. That will keep money from becoming an idol in our heart.

SOUL SEARCH: How can I trust God more than I already do?

**Father, I trust you with my whole heart.
Amen.**

PROUD LIKE PEACOCKS

Before destruction the heart of man is haughty,
and before honor is humility.

—PROVERBS 18:12

*L*ife has a way of humbling the proudest of us, and that's good because the proud and haughty don't think very deeply. They are so consumed with their own self-importance that they don't think of how life is full of coming storms.

How we should pity the haughty, the arrogant, and the proud sinner. They distance themselves from God because of their love of sin, yet God is the only one who can save them from the ultimate storms of death and damnation in hell. We should pity them because we were once proud and haughty. We were once consumed with our own sense of self-importance, and, like peacocks, we were vainly puffed up in our own minds.

But God was "rich in mercy" toward us (Ephesians 2:4). Perhaps He led some humble soul to cry out for our salvation. May we do the same for others.

SOUL SEARCH: When was the last time I became puffed up by my own abilities?

**Father, thank you for your patience with me.
Amen.**

A GOOD HEARER

He who answers a matter before he hears it,
it is folly and shame to him.

—PROVERBS 18:13

*H*ow easy it is to be one who answers before we hear a matter. We offer a solution before we hear the problem. How frustrating for the person with the problem. A good hearer will listen with patience and then give advice.

This is not only important when listening to a brother or sister who is sharing a problem and needs a listening ear, but also to an unsaved person who is sharing his worn-out and erroneous beliefs. When we hear a sinner tell us how evolution has proof, or that Noah's ark couldn't have happened, it's easy to become impatient and overtalk them. Scripture reminds us to be patient when instructing those who oppose themselves.

The key is to know our agenda. We are to listen with patience and then to look for opportunity to share the gospel.

SOUL SEARCH: When was the last time impatience caused me to answer before the question was asked?

∽

Father, please help me to be a good listener.
Amen.

SERIOUS WOUNDS

The spirit of a man will sustain him in sickness,
but who can bear a broken spirit?

—PROVERBS 18:14

We have all had physical wounds—from a skinned knee as a child, to a cut finger, to more serious wounds. We instinctively know that to heal any wound we need to cleanse it, bandage it, and protect it.

We know how to treat a wounded body, but we don't know how to tend a wounded spirit. Demonic oppression can wound our spirit. The apostle Paul was buffeted by an angel of Satan and couldn't tend to himself, so he pleaded with God for deliverance, and for reasons only known to God, it didn't come.

Perhaps a wounded spirit has left you bewildered and oppressed by fear. Then trust God to stop the lion's mouth. He will take you through rather than pull you out, because He is at work in you to will and do of His good pleasure. He said to Paul in the midst of his trial, "My grace is sufficient for you" (2 Corinthians 12:9). It is for us also.

SOUL SEARCH: When is one time when my spirit was wounded by another person? How was God's grace sufficient in the situation?

**Father, please help me to forgive and forget
any transgression against me. Amen.**

September 16

LIFE-SAVING KNOWLEDGE

The heart of the prudent acquires knowledge,
and the ear of the wise seeks knowledge.

—PROVERBS 18:15

You've just arrived in a hotel, and so you study the diagram on the wall in your room to get knowledge of how to escape if there is a fire. You know that in a blinding, smoke-filled environment, knowledge can save you from perishing.

Hosea 4:6 tells us that God Himself warned that His people perish because of a lack of knowledge of His law. The ear of the wise seeks such knowledge, because it brings us to the One who can save us from hell. Scripture says that the law is a schoolmaster to bring us to Christ (Galatians 3:24 AKJV).

May God help us to follow the example of Jesus, as He opened the moral law in the Sermon on the Mount. It is the spiritual nature of law that gives us the necessary knowledge to see our need for God's mercy in Christ.

SOUL SEARCH: If death were to take me today, would I be ready to face God? Why or why not?

Father, let me be trusting alone in Jesus today for my eternal salvation. Amen.

September 17

DO SOMETHING

A man's gift makes room for him,
and brings him before great men.
—PROVERBS 18:16

Those who can run fast do so when they find themselves a step ahead of the rest. Those who find that they can write soon put a serious pen to paper, and those who can talk soon have good things to say and are asked by others to say them. Our gifts make room for us in our natural life as well as in the spiritual realm. But in both cases, those who can run must run, those who can write must write, and those who can talk must talk.

Do you desire God's gifts? Then begin using what you already have, in faith. Help others. Pray. Encourage people. Preach. Give. Sing. Talk. Share your faith with the unsaved despite your fears. Don't pray for less fear; pray for more love.

It's then that your gifting will become apparent. It is then that your gift will make room for you and bring you before great men.

SOUL SEARCH: What are some of the gifts God has given me? Have I ever felt like God forgot to gift me?

*Father, as I step out and trust you, may the gifts
you have given me become apparent. Amen.*

September 18

HE THAT IS FIRST

He that is first in his own cause seems just;
but his neighbor comes and searches him.
—PROVERBS 18:17 AKJV

*I*f you've ever watched a court program on TV, you will know that he who is first to present his case has us believing that his opponent is guilty. But when the opponent testifies, the information he brings changes our minds.

Here's another example of the power of information to change our minds: Would you like a large bottle of fresh water or $10 million? You can only choose one. Now here is some missing information that could change your mind: you are alone in the middle of a massive hot and dry desert.

The world is ignorant of God's righteousness, and so they wrongly think all is well between themselves and heaven. That's why we need to give them information that will radically change their minds—at the moment they are choosing the riches of sin rather than the pure waters of righteousness. So put them in a desert.

God's moral law was designed to do just that (Romans 3:19–20; 7:7, 13; Galatians 3:24). Use it as Jesus did to bring information (the knowledge of sin), and that will cause them to thirst for the righteousness that is alone in Christ.

SOUL SEARCH: Have I enough love to reach out to the unsaved? What fears do I need to overcome to do so?

Father, please help me to see that my fears are nothing compared to the fate of the ungodly. Amen.

September 19

TAILS, I WIN

Casting lots causes contentions to cease,
and keeps the mighty apart.
—PROVERBS 18:18

*C*asting lots is referenced seven times in the New Testament and seventy times in the Old Testament—always as a way of settling disputes. Not mentioned is what was being cast. The lots may have been sticks cut to various lengths (such as drawing straws) or flat stones or some sort of dice.

The contemporary form of casting lots would be tossing a coin, perhaps the most famous being the coin toss before the NFL's Super Bowl event. Whatever form the toss takes, it's designed to cause contention between two teams to cease and keeps the mighty apart from each other.

As Christians, we need not cast lots because God's Word is a "lamp to [our] feet and a light to [our] path" (Psalm 119:105). Its principles show us which direction to take.

SOUL SEARCH: Do I know God's will through study of His Word?

**Father, may I always choose to take
the paths of righteousness. Amen.**

September 20

AN OFFENDED BROTHER

A brother offended is harder to win than a strong city,
and contentions are like the bars of a castle.

—PROVERBS 18:19

*I*f anyone had occasion to be an offended brother, it was Jacob's son Joseph. His brothers hated his many-colored coat, and motivated by envy, they betrayed him and sold him into slavery. He was falsely accused, and in due time rose to a place of honor. The tears come when we see how much he loved his brothers, and how he held no bitterness for their terrible betrayal.

The wonder of the narrative is even greater when we see that Joseph was a type of Christ, who was betrayed, delivered to the Romans because of his envious brethren, and sold for thirty pieces of silver, and who cried out, "Father, forgive them" (Luke 23:34). He then rose to the ultimate place of honor seated on the right hand of God.

We are to strive to be like our Savior, and be so filled with the love of God that we let nothing offend us but sin.

SOUL SEARCH: Do I search the Scriptures, or do I read them out of some sort of obligation?

**Father, open my eyes to the wonderful truths
hidden in your Word. Amen.**

September 21

FORGETTING TO EAT

A man's stomach shall be satisfied from the fruit of his mouth;
from the produce of his lips he shall be filled.

—PROVERBS 18:20

*H*ave you ever been so passionate about something or enjoyed doing something so much that you forgot to eat?

Jesus told His disciples that He had food to eat of which they knew nothing. His food was to do the will of God (John 4:32–34). That was what His appetite craved, and that's what gave Him His satisfaction.

There is a great feeling of satisfaction for those who regularly share their faith with dying sinners. And how wonderful it is that God chose to bring the message of everlasting life to human beings through weak and lowly human lips.

May God give us wisdom and increase our lips to take the glorious gospel of Jesus Christ into a dark world.

SOUL SEARCH: What is my "food"? Is it to do the will of God?

Father, let my will be your will. Amen.

September 22

MADE BY THE WORD

Death and life are in the power of the tongue,
and those who love it will eat its fruit.

—PROVERBS 18:21

Words are powerful. God created the heavens and the earth with them when He said, "Let there be light" (Genesis 1:3). And there was light. Scripture says "all things were made through Him" (John 1:3).

When God walked this earth in the person of Jesus Christ, there was life in His words. They brought life back to the four-days-dead body of Lazarus when He said, "Lazarus, come forth" (John 11:43).

Today we can use our words to create or destroy, to speak words of life or of death, to build up or tear down, or to speak words that have positive or negative repercussions. But the best thing we can do with our tongue today is use it to bring the life of the glorious gospel to dying sinners. May the love of God help us to conquer our fears and speak words of life today.

SOUL SEARCH: Would people say I'm a positive person or a negative person? Why?

*Father, help me see everything as positive for me,
in the light of Romans 8:28. Amen.*

September 23

THE GOOD THING

He who finds a wife finds a good thing,
and obtains favor from the LORD.
—PROVERBS 18:22

It's not good for a man to be alone (Genesis 2:18). In the beginning God created woman for man and man for woman. Then He joined them together in holy matrimony.

When a man and a woman are joined in marriage, they become one flesh and have the ability to be like God and reproduce their own kind. We take it for granted that we can make human beings in our likeness. So often children not only look like their parents, but they talk and act like them.

We know marriage is, in reality, a picture of Christ and His bride, the church. It was a "good thing" when Jesus found us and brought us to Himself. From the moment of our conception at new birth—when the seed of the Word of God was planted in us—God has been at work in us to conform us "to the image of His Son" (Romans 8:29).

SOUL SEARCH: Am I more like Jesus today than I was yesterday? What can I do so that I am more like Jesus tomorrow than I was today?

∽

**Father, please conform me to the image
of your Son. Amen.**

WITHOUT PRICE

The poor man uses entreaties,
but the rich answers roughly.

—PROVERBS 18:23

*T*he rich don't need to use discretion or politeness when they want something, because their riches speak for them. They get anything they want because everything has a price. Everything, that is, except eternal life—that is without price.

The Bible says, "No man can by any means redeem his brother" (Psalm 49:7 NASB). This is because the price for our redemption from death was too high. Nothing we could offer God would have turned away His wrath from sin. So God, who is rich in mercy, provided the payment for us.

Then, as we look back on the cross, we say with the apostle Peter, "[We] were not redeemed with corruptible things, like silver or gold … but with the precious blood of Christ" (1 Peter 1:18–20). And we warn the rich that they too need the Savior, and that they won't be answering roughly on the day of judgment, because, "riches do not profit in the day of wrath, but righteousness delivers from death" (Proverbs 11:4).

SOUL SEARCH: Have I ever unconsciously shown favor to the rich? If so, why?

**Father, help me to be no respecter of persons.
Amen.**

September 25

THICKER THAN WATER

A man who has friends must himself be friendly,
but there is a friend who sticks closer than a brother.
—PROVERBS 18:24

*F*riendly people have many friends. If you're not outgoing and you don't make friends very easily, learn from those who do. Watch how they show a genuine interest in other people. See how they ask them about themselves and make them feel at ease by getting them to talk about their interests.

Friendly people also often give gifts. Who doesn't like someone who does that? It's a practical and evident way to show others that you appreciate them.

It is true that blood is thicker than water. Brothers and sisters tend to stick close to each other. But there is a Friend who sticks closer than family. We have a friend in Jesus, who loves us with endless love that proved itself in dying for us. He will never leave us or forsake us (Deuteronomy 31:6).

SOUL SEARCH: Am I a friendly person? Do I show a genuine interest in others, or do I tend to talk about myself?

**Father, make me a friendly person for
the gospel's sake. Amen.**

IMPRESSIVE INSTRUCTIONS

Better is the poor who walks in his integrity,
than one who is perverse in his lips,
and is a fool.

—PROVERBS 19:1

Those who use filthy language to express themselves have perverse lips. The poor man who walks in his integrity is better than someone who, like a dumb sheep, goes astray and turns to his own way.

The ones who have integrity keep to the moral path. No matter what tries to turn them away from what is good, they stay the course.

That's the nature of the godly. We should always return to our integrity. We should always do what is right and good. We stubbornly keep our integrity when this perverse world tries to bend and twist us from the path of righteousness.

SOUL SEARCH: Is there any temptation that would cause me to compromise my integrity? If so, how can I overcome that?

**Father, may I be uncompromisingly godly,
always walking in the fear of the Lord. Amen.**

HASTY DECISIONS

Also it is not good for a soul to be without knowledge,
and he sins who hastens with his feet.
—PROVERBS 19:2

*H*ow tragic it is to think of how many people have hastened to take their own life when a good night's sleep and the dawn of a new morning could have changed their mind about ending their life.

Beware of any hasty decisions—of fast marriages, quick deals, and thoughtless promises. Humility of heart understands that, as human beings, we continually make wrong decisions, and that we must think things through before making important choices.

The key with every decision in life is not to ask, "What would Jesus do?" This is because our wickedness of heart can make Him do anything it wants Him to do. It is safer to ask, "What *did* Jesus do?" and "What does God say about the subject in His Word?"

Before making any decision, always ask what God's Word says, and if you're not clear, seek godly advice from someone who walks in the fear of the Lord.

SOUL SEARCH: When was the last time I was impetuous? What did I learn from the result?

*Father, remind me to wait on you and refrain
from hasty decisions. Amen.*

A LICK OF WISDOM

The foolishness of a man twists his way,
and his heart frets against the LORD.
—PROVERBS 19:3

Show me a man who denies the existence of God, and I will show you a man who loves his sin more than reason and truth. Show me a man who blasphemes God's name, and I will show you a man who lacks even a lick of wisdom.

Blasphemy is evidence that the Bible is true, when it says that the sinful mind of man is in a state of hostility toward God (Romans 8:7). It even gives us the cause of the hostility: the moral law. The law stirs up the nature of sin. It shines a light on the cockroaches in the dark and dirty cellar of the human heart.

The more a nation perverts its way, the more it will blaspheme the name of God and be hostile toward the gospel and those who live righteously in Christ Jesus. But we need not be discouraged. The darker it gets, the brighter the light of the gospel will shine. Where sin abounds, there does much more grace abound. May God help us to reach the lost while there is still time.

SOUL SEARCH: Am I horrified by blasphemy, or do I overlook it?

Father, cause me to be jealous for your name, and to have the courage to lovingly refute those who dishonor it.
Amen.

September 29

EVIDENT LOVE

Wealth makes many friends,
but the poor is separated from his friend.
—PROVERBS 19:4

They say it's possible to make sixty-seven words out of the word *wealth*. Wealth can also make many friends. King Solomon knew that. The Queen of Sheba and many others came for a friendly visit to see his riches and hear his wisdom.

Perhaps, like me, you're not wealthy, but you have some spare change. Then do what I do. I purchase a stack of $5 Subway gift cards, and I give one or two to everyone with whom I share the gospel. It is so good to say to a stranger, "Hey, thanks for listening to me. Here's a small gift for you." To give a practical gift to a lost person is to give them a small token of genuine love.

I know that if someone shared the gospel with me before I was a Christian and topped it off with even a small gift card, I would never forget it. Nor would I be too quick to dismiss what they said.

SOUL SEARCH: Am I a fisher of men? If not, what steps can I take to become one?

Father, help me to follow in the footsteps of Jesus.
Amen.

CROCKER MEN

A false witness will not go unpunished,
and he who speaks lies will not escape.

—PROVERBS 19:5

*I*t's been often said that taking the easiest path is what makes men and rivers crooked. If you see a river from high in the sky, you will see that it twists and turns around every obstacle.

The liar, like Jacob in the Bible, twists and turns to avoid moral responsibility. And what great trouble Jacob brought to himself with his lies to his father. And what grief his sons brought to him in his old age, when they lied to him about Joseph. Jacob reproduced more of his own kind.

What great cost there was to Ananias and Sapphira, when they lied to the Holy Spirit and were struck dead!

May each of us learn from liars in Scripture, fear God, and always speak the truth knowing that liars will not escape. They will certainly end up in hell if they don't repent and trust the Savior.

SOUL SEARCH: What life lessons have I learned from Scripture?

**Father, daily teach me, guide me,
and speak to me from your Word. Amen.**

Think on These Things

WISDOM
FOR LIFE
FROM
Proverbs

RAY COMFORT

BroadStreet
PUBLISHING

BroadStreet Publishing® Group, LLC
Savage, Minnesota USA
BroadStreetPublishing.com

Think on These Things: WISDOM FOR LIFE FROM PROVERBS

Stock or custom editions of BroadStreet Publishing titles may be purchased in bulk for educational, business, ministry, fundraising, or sales promotional use. For information, please e-mail info@broadstreetpublishing.com.

Cover design by Chris Garborg/garborgdesign.com
Typeset by Katherine Lloyd/theDESKonline.com

Printed in China

19 20 21 22 23 24 6 5 4 3 2 1

October

October 1

DOUBLE GRIEF

Many entreat the favor of the nobility,
and every man is a friend to one who gives gifts.

—PROVERBS 19:6

Think of how many will plead for favor from the Prince of Life when they stand in terror before Him—when He judges the world in righteousness. But on that day it will be too late. They rejected His mercy when it was offered, and now they will reap the harsh judgment of His law. But the anguish will be in that sinners will not only miss out on heaven; they will also reap hell. That is double grief.

By going through the moral law with the lost, we can (with the help of God) cause them to entreat the favor of God offered in Christ. Only those who realize that they need mercy will seek it.

If everyone is a friend to him who gives gifts, how much more does God become our Friend when He gives us the gift of everlasting life? The apostle Paul called it the "indescribable gift" (1 Corinthians 9:15).

SOUL SEARCH: What does it mean to be "acquainted with grief" (Isaiah 53:3) like Jesus was? Am I acquainted with this grief?

Father, help me to walk each day with a godly empathy for the unsaved. Amen.

THE POWER OF HYPERBOLE

All the brothers of the poor hate him;
how much more do his friends go far from him!
He may pursue them with words, yet they abandon him.

—PROVERBS 19:7

*H*yperbole is commonly used in Scripture. It employs the politically incorrect and powerful word *hate* for the sake of emphasis.

The Bible says that if you don't correct your children when they do wrong, you hate them (Proverbs 13:24). In other words, you may as well hate them because you certainly don't love them enough to teach right from wrong.

The Bible also says that you should so love God, that all of your affections—your love for your mother, father, brother, sister, wife, husband, and children—should seem like hatred compared to the love you have for the God who gave them to you. Hyperbole has the effect of shocking us into reality.

Humanity certainly needs to be shocked into reality. We should discipline our children and teach them right from wrong if we truly love them. We should love God with all of our heart, soul, and strength (Deuteronomy 6:5) because He gave us life, and His being first in our affections is therefore good and right.

SOUL SEARCH: How does my love for God compare to my love for all other things? Does the love I have for God make my love for other things seem like hatred?

Father, may I love you more dearly each day. Amen.

October 3

DO YOURSELF A FAVOR

He who gets wisdom loves his own soul;
he who keeps understanding will find good.
—PROVERBS 19:8

A day doesn't go by when I don't pray for wisdom, and a day doesn't go by when I don't need it.

If you want to do yourself a favor, pray for wisdom. If you love your own soul, pray for wisdom, because, as the Bible says, wisdom is the principal thing (Proverbs 4:7). It's on top of the list.

If you have the wisdom of God, you will always think right, you will always do the right thing, and you will always say what is right. The Bible also says that if we lack wisdom, we simply need to ask God and He will give it to us liberally (James 1:5). Solomon found out that God keeps that promise, and when he asked God for wisdom it greatly pleased the Lord (1 Kings 3:10).

The Scriptures say he who wins souls is wise (Proverbs 11:30). So be wise today, seek God for wisdom, and then use that wisdom to seek and save those who are lost. There is no wiser way to spend your life.

SOUL SEARCH: What do I esteem as the principle thing? Is it wisdom?

⌒

**Father, make me wise by giving me the spirit of wisdom.
Help me daily to do the right thing. Amen.**

DNA EVIDENCE

A false witness will not go unpunished,
and he who speaks lies shall perish.
—PROVERBS 19:9

A false witness is a particularly despicable liar. This is because his lying is specifically against someone for an alleged crime, and because of his false witness an innocent person may be found guilty, go to prison, or even be put to death. Whether or not that happens, the false witness shall not go unpunished, because God's just wrath will eventually come upon him.

In recent years, DNA evidence has shown us that it is not uncommon for innocent people to spend decades in prison. Some have lost their lives because someone bore false witness in court. Such wickedness wouldn't take place if people feared God. The Scriptures tell us that "by the fear of the LORD one departs from evil" (Proverbs 16:6).

Those who fear God will always speak the truth, because they seek God's smile rather than His frown. And they know that His frown will result in damnation in a terrible place called hell.

SOUL SEARCH: Do I speak the truth in love (Ephesians 4:15), or do I say what other people want to hear?

**Father, may I love you, hate sin, and speak the truth
of the gospel without fear. Amen.**

BIGGER AND BETTER

Delight is not seemly for a fool;
much less for a servant to have rule over princes.

—PROVERBS 19:10

*D*elight isn't good for a fool, because his delight is only in what is foolish.

The Bible says that if we delight ourselves in the Lord, He will give us our heart's desires (Psalm 37:4). However, that wonderful verse has been abused by those whose desires are not godly. Their desires are fueled by greed; they want more, bigger, and better.

But when we are born again, we say, "The LORD is my shepherd; I shall not want" (Psalm 23:1). We crucify that sinful flesh with all of its wants. Now, above all else, we desire only what pleases God. We seek Him to give us a hunger for His Word, a closer walk, and a deep desire to do His will.

So when we delight ourselves in the Lord, we can be assured that He will then give us our heart's desires, because His will has become our will.

SOUL SEARCH: Do I still "want," or am I satisfied in the Lord?

⁀◦

Father, let all my want be satisfied in you.
Amen.

October 6

DEFERRED ANGER

The discretion of a man makes him slow to anger,
and his glory is to overlook a transgression.
—PROVERBS 19:11

The Bible says to "be angry, and do not sin" (Psalm 4:4). It's okay to be angry. Certain social issues should stir up a righteous indignation in the godly.

However, tailgaters cause me to be angry and I want to sin. They remind me that I'm a wretched sinner. I see them in my rearview mirror, coming up behind my car as though there's no tomorrow. Then they sit on my tail, almost always in an SUV that's so big it would hardly be damaged if it plowed into the back of my little VW, wrecked it, and sent me to the hospital or the morgue. What makes me angry is the fact that they almost certainly couldn't stop if I put my brakes on hard. But they trust in their abilities at my expense.

So what should the godly do about tailgaters? Change lanes. We defer our anger and let the transgressor pass. The alternative is to transgress our conscience, or perhaps end up a victim of road rage. There's a lesson there for the rest of life also: Move over and let angry people pass.

SOUL SEARCH: When was the last time I got angry while driving? Do I drive with the Golden Rule in mind?

$\backsim$

**Father, help me to treat others as I would
like to be treated. Amen.**

A ROARING LION

The king's wrath is like the roaring of a lion,
but his favor is like dew on the grass.

—PROVERBS 19:12

If the king's wrath is as terrifying as the roaring of a lion, how much more terrifying is the wrath of God! Yet we rarely hear preachers warning a sinful world that the wrath of God abides on them (John 3:36) or that they are "by nature children of wrath" (Ephesians 2:3).

But we can't in good conscience divorce ourselves from the doctrine. The Scriptures are thoroughly laced with warnings of God's justice. Romans 2:5 warns that when we sin, we store up wrath that will be revealed on judgment day. How they will wish that we warned them!

The greatest example of wrath isn't seen in the dealings of God with Israel or with any individual; it is seen in His justice as it fell on the innocent Lamb of God. His wrath fell on Him so that it wouldn't fall on us. He experienced justice so that we could experience mercy, and He tasted death so that we could relish the taste of everlasting life.

SOUL SEARCH: How can I show God daily that I appreciate his mercy toward me?

**Father, thank you for your everlasting mercy.
Amen.**

WHEN PETALS FALL

A foolish son is the ruin of his father,
and the contentions of a wife are a continual dropping.
—PROVERBS 19:13

*M*ost men are pretty superficial. They pick the flower for its color and not its fragrance. Many a man has found that he hasn't been left with too much, when in time the petals fall. A wise man rather chooses a wife by the fragrance of a godly character. He looks for the "fruit of the Spirit" (Galatians 5:22)—things like love, joy, peace, goodness, gentleness, meekness, patience. These are the virtues that please God.

Hollywood epitomizes godless superficiality. Looks are chosen above character, and divorces are as common as fleas on mangy dogs. In time, the Hollywood husband strays like a dog with no leash. "Irreconcilable differences," they say.

That's why Christian teens should be encouraged to choose spouses at 6:00 a.m. on the second morning of youth camp. The petals aren't so prevalent that hour of the morning.

SOUL SEARCH: Do I judge people by their character or by their looks?

**Father, help me to shun superficiality.
Amen.**

October 9

WEALTH AND POVERTY

House and riches are an inheritance from fathers,
but a prudent wife is from the LORD.
—PROVERBS 19:14

*I*t's been often said that where there's a will, there's a relative. It's also true that lottery winners have instant friends. Lots of friendly, wanton friends. Everyone appreciates having a little extra cash, and if a rich man slips some your way when things are tough, even an atheist would secretly thank God.

Some say that wealth brings many problems, but don't let anyone convince you that poverty has less. It is good for a man to be in a position financially to provide a house for his family. It is good for him to have money in the bank to pay bills, support his local church, support overseas missionaries, and give to the poor. And it's good for him to leave an inheritance to his children.

SOUL SEARCH: What Christian causes do I aid? Are there any others that the Lord is leading me to support?

Father, thank you that you supply all of my needs according to your riches in glory. Amen.

October 10

LAZY DOGS

Slothfulness casts one into a deep sleep,
and an idle person will suffer hunger.
—PROVERBS 19:15

Christians have no excuse for laziness. We are instead to be always abounding in the work of the Lord (1 Corinthians 15:58). We are soldiers of Christ, and no army wants warriors who lie around like lazy dogs. Instead, they want those who are fit, not fat—those who are trained to shake off the slack of sloth and "fight the good fight of faith" (1 Timothy 6:12).

The key to doing anything in this life is to be diligent to do all things "as to the Lord" (Colossians 3:23)—not to love sleep, but to instead use it as a means to rest a body weary with labor. The Bible also likens the godly to athletes running a race (1 Corinthians 9:24). No runner who has a lazy mind will finish the course. So our attitude should always be to strive to run our race, because the world only runs for an earthly crown. But we run for an eternal one (v. 25).

SOUL SEARCH: Am I abounding in the work of the Lord, or do I sometimes get lazy?

**Father, help me to run the Christian race
with divine energy. Amen.**

EARNED WAGES

He who keeps the commandment keeps his soul;
but he who is careless of his ways will die.

—PROVERBS 19:16

*T*he law says, "Do this and you will live" (Luke 10:28). The problem is that if we violate the law, the wages for breaking it is death. In the book of Romans, the apostle Paul opined how his hope for salvation was in the law. But the commandments brought death to him, because he continually violated their perfect precepts.

Millions are deceived into thinking that the Ten Commandments are a moral standard we are to strive to keep. But the moral law was given instead to show us our sin. It's a mirror that reflects what we are in truth—that we are all like "an unclean thing" (Isaiah 64:6).

The greatest favor we could ever do for any human being is to hold up the mirror for them to see themselves, as Jesus did in the greatest of all sermons. In doing so, the law does what it was designed to do: be "our schoolmaster to bring us unto Christ" (Galatians 3:24 AKJV).

SOUL SEARCH: Do I regularly hold up the mirror of the moral law for sinners to see themselves as God sees them? Do I hold it up for myself?

Father, please give me divine encounters—people whom you have prepared to hear the words of life. Amen.

PITY THE POOR

He who has pity upon the poor lends to the LORD,
and He will pay back what he has given.

—PROVERBS 19:17

*T*hose who have once been poor can best pity the poor. Those who haven't been poor can only imagine what it must be like to have to scrape for every meal, to lack money for clothing, to have little hope of owning a home, and to have a very real fear that one day you and your precious family may be homeless.

But the Christian has the love of God shed abroad in his heart, and he therefore gives because empathy is tied to love. He who is able to give to the poor "lends to the LORD." In other words, if we give to the poor, God in His great kindness considers our gift as His debt, and the inference is that He will pay us back even though giving to the poor wasn't a loan.

We may believe that the poor are the only beneficiaries, but we are also benefitting, because in our giving we are both trusting and pleasing God, and that is to our benefit.

SOUL SEARCH: In what ways do I care for the poor?

**Father, help me to be responsible for that with
which you have entrusted me. Amen.**

A SMALL SPARK

Chasten your son while there is hope,
and do not set your heart on his destruction.

—PROVERBS 19:18

Those who wait until the teenage years to chasten their kids are trying to close the gate after the horse has gone. Rebellion is like a small spark in a dry forest. Those who think it's no big deal are either very foolish or partially insane. A small spark can in moments become an inferno that can do millions of dollars of damage—or even take human lives.

This is why those who don't put out the spark of rebellion in their toddlers are foolish. Rebellion in kids is not funny or cute. It won't be too long until the spark becomes a large fire that can do great damage to your child and to others. Then hope is gone. There is only a limited time in which we can chasten our children.

Ignore what the godless world says. If you instead listen to what the Word of God says, the time will come when your godly teenager gives you great joy and not pain.

SOUL SEARCH: Am I ever flippant about that which God says is very serious? If so, what and why?

⌒

**Father, cause me to take to heart any
warning in your Word. Amen.**

October 14

IMPRESSIVE TESTIMONY

A man of great wrath shall suffer punishment;
for if you rescue him, you will have to do it again.

—PROVERBS 19:19

This verse reminds me of an experience that taught me a valuable lesson. I once met a young man who had an impressive testimony. He said he was Jewish and came from a huge family, and he sure could talk. When we baptized him, even his coming out of the water was impressive. He was like a whale bursting through the surface of the ocean.

But after a while we noticed that he had a serious anger problem with people in our church, at one point even threatening to kill me. That's when this verse became meaningful to me.

He then stole a widow's car and ran off with the collection bag. When the police caught him, they found he had a huge rap sheet that included multiple counts of arson. The experience taught me not to be impressed with leaves and branches, but to look for biblical fruit in those who profess faith in Jesus.

SOUL SEARCH: What impresses me in people? Am I ever impressed by preachers who are gifted but lack godly fruit in their lives?

∽

**Father, help me to recognize wolves in sheep's clothing
(Matthew 7:15). Amen.**

October 15

DESPITE THE WARNING

Listen to counsel and receive instruction,
that you may be wise in your latter days.
—PROVERBS 19:20

Toddlers think they know best, until their incessant touching and climbing results in bruises—or they find that the heater really does burn. The teenager thinks he knows best when he experiments with heroin despite the warning of his parents, and he ends up dying a painful death on a restroom floor. Or the sweet teenager thinks she knows best when she ignores the instruction of her mother, who pleaded with her to hold onto her virginity, and she ends up killing her own precious child while it's still in her womb.

Counsel surrounds us in the form of those who love us, in the voice of our conscience, and in the Word of God. But human nature so often ignores these protections and reaps pain and suffering.

May we always listen to the wisdom that will keep us on the path of righteousness, because that's the only thing that will matter in the latter days.

SOUL SEARCH: Do I value the voice of my conscience, or do I follow the world's advice?

Father, give me a sensitive ear to wise counsel.
Amen.

October 16

EVERYTHING IS TRANSIENT

There are many plans in a man's heart,
nevertheless the LORD's counsel—that will stand.

—PROVERBS 19:21

Nothing is permanent, except God and what He says. Everything else is temporary and subject to corruption. Even the sun isn't permanent. This massive earth fits into the volume of the sun a million times, but in time the massively huge sun will burn out and turn to stardust.

But the word of the Lord will last forever (Isaiah 40:8), and the Bible says that all who trust in the Savior have everlasting life. They will be part of a kingdom of which "there will be no end" (Luke 1:33).

His promises are immutable. Trust them with all of your heart. He will never go back on what He says will take place. It shall stand. This is so very reassuring in a world where we are forever disappointed by other people's promises, despite good intentions.

SOUL SEARCH: In what do I find my security? Do I cling to God for my very life?

◡◠

**Father, thank you that you keep every
promise you make. Amen.**

October 17

A LITTLE KINDNESS

What is desired in a man is kindness,
and a poor man is better than a liar.

—PROVERBS 19:22

There are differing interpretations of the first part of this verse. Some think that it is referring to a man who is truly desiring to show kindness to others, while others think it is referring to a rich man who desires to use his wealth to be a blessing to others. No doubt that such is the testimony of every Christian who has the love of God within them, to have money enough to help others who are in need.

We see this benevolence immediately manifest itself with Zacchaeus, who, the moment he came to the Savior, said that if he had wronged anyone, he would pay them back fourfold (Luke 19:8). Imagine what a shock that would have been to those he had overtaxed, to have that little man come to the door and with a big heart say, "I have put my faith in Jesus of Nazareth, so here is four times the amount I overtaxed you."

May we also shock this world with kindness.

SOUL SEARCH: When was the last time I made an effort to right a wrong I had done to another?

~๑~

**Father, let me go the extra mile with others.
Amen.**

THE CATALYST

The fear of the LORD leads to life,
and he who has it will abide in satisfaction;
he will not be visited with evil.

—PROVERBS 19:23

*T*his is the verse that I often include when I sign books. It says that fearing God causes us to live. Surely there is no truth greater than the one that tells us how to keep away from death.

That's what the fear of God does. It is the catalyst that causes us to depart from evil so that we can live. It is the motivation for repentance. The Scriptures speak of "repentance unto life" (Acts 11:18 KJV).

Then we are told that if we have the fear of the Lord, we will remain satisfied. Isn't this what we are seeking when we drink, eat, or buy something? We are seeking to be satisfied. And third, if we fear God, we will not be visited with evil. Who in their right mind would want evil to visit them? So who in their right mind wouldn't desperately want to cultivate the fear of the Lord?

SOUL SEARCH: Do I cultivate the fear of the Lord? If so, how?

**Father, help me to understand your power
and your holy nature. Amen.**

SPIRITUAL ANOREXIA

A lazy man buries his hand in the bowl,
and will not so much as bring it to his mouth again.

—PROVERBS 19:24

It is truly a lazy man who finds it painful to exert energy to eat. Even a sloth has a good appetite. God has put an instinct to eat within His entire creation, but some dull that desire and find themselves deceived by anorexia.

God forbid that from happening spiritually. May we never be so lazy that we don't bother to feed on the Word of God every day! We are to desire the sincere milk of the Word as newborn babes (1 Peter 2:2), and if the desire isn't there, best we feed on it anyway, in case we become spiritually anorexic.

The tragedy with physical anorexia is that the skeletal victim looks in the mirror and sees the problem, but is helpless to do anything about it. The same can happen spiritually. Sin can steal our health, and without the grace of God we are helpless to do anything about it. Jesus said that if we serve sin, we are a slave to it (see John 8:34). That's why we need to cry, "Search me, O God … try me, and know my anxieties; and see if there is any wicked way in me" (Psalm 139:23–24).

SOUL SEARCH: Do I discipline myself to read God's Word daily? If not, what do I need to do to start?

∽

**Father, give me an insatiable appetite
for the Scriptures. Amen.**

NO SIGN OF THE LAW

Strike a scoffer, and the simple will become wary;
rebuke one who has understanding,
and he will discern knowledge.

—PROVERBS 19:25

*H*ave you ever been driving on the freeway and noticed that when a police car is present, the citizens become law abiding? Yet when there is no sign of the law, almost everyone speeds. The United States has lost sight of God's law, and the result is that there are few who fear God, and when that happens almost everyone rushes into lawlessness.

However, the day will come when the law will smite those who scorn. It will fall upon those who say that God doesn't see and that He won't seek retribution.

On that terrifying day, those who are meek and have trusted the simple gospel will beware. In the meantime, let's pray that there are those who can understand what we are trying to say when we share the knowledge of God.

SOUL SEARCH: What consequences have I faced in the past for sinning? Would I give myself to the pleasures of sin if there were no repercussions?

Father, I am so thankful for your patience,
mercy, and grace. Amen.

RETRIBUTION

He who mistreats his father and chases away his mother
is a son who causes shame and brings reproach.

—PROVERBS 19:26

"*H*onor your father and your mother" (Exodus 20:12) is the first commandment given with a promise (Ephesians 6:1–2). We tend to think that promises are positive, but this one is a promise of retribution. It comes with a threat, saying that if you don't honor your parents, your days will not be long upon the earth and all will not be well with you.

We live among a generation that has given itself to sin. It's one that is openly rebellious toward their parents and is given to demons that seduce many into drink and drugs. And it's one that often ends in a shortened life. All is not well with them, and their days are not long upon the earth.

According to the American Foundation for Suicide Prevention, there are an average of 121 suicides per day.* This is a tragedy, and one that should cause those of us who love God to plead with Him to use us to reach these people before they make the terrible decision to take their own lives.

SOUL SEARCH: When was a time when I was tempted to (or did) not honor my parents? Do I honor them now?

∽◦

**Father, help me to honor my parents
because you tell me to honor them. Amen.**

---

* "Suicide Statistics," American Foundation for Suicide Prevention, https://afsp.org/about-suicide/suicide-statistics/.

October 22

DON'T LISTEN

Cease listening to instruction, my son,
and you will stray from the words of knowledge.
—PROVERBS 19:27

*D*on't listen to this world's advice. Cease to hear them.
Stop your ears. They are wrong about child discipline,
about the nature of marriage, about women's rights, about when
to forgive, and about the nature of God, the deity of Jesus, and
a million and one other vital issues.

Psalm 1:1 promises God's blessing on us if we don't listen
to the world's suggestions. The world will tell you to keep your
religion to yourself and not push it on others. They will tell you
not to talk about hell and sin, and they will insist that people
are morally good.

The Bible says the opposite. We are to preach the gospel to
every person, in season and out of season (2 Timothy 4:2), and
because of love we are to confront sinners about sin and warn
them of the reality of hell. So resolve to not listen to anything
that causes you to turn away from the instruction of the Word
of God.

SOUL SEARCH: Am I hesitant to say that I believe the
Bible, or am I completely unashamed?

*Father, never let me waver over the words of Scripture.
Jesus said that your Word is truth. Amen.*

FAMISHED MALES

A disreputable witness scorns judgment,
and the mouth of the wicked devours iniquity.

—PROVERBS 19:28

*T*he wicked do drink iniquity like water. They devour sin like a hungry animal. Jesus said that they love the darkness and hate the light (John 3:19–20).

Years ago, a major TV network adequately confirmed this by boasting that through their entertainment they guaranteed to break more commandments than any other TV network. Such advertising brings in hungry viewers like a barbecue attracts famished males. The New Testament describes the sinful as "having eyes full of adultery" (2 Peter 2:14). How can we deny such an accurate description of the nature of man?

Yet when someone dies, it's as though they were morally perfect. The eulogies paint a picture of the most incredibly good, wonderfully kind, super nice, fantastically friendly, and tremendously generous person who ever lived.

SOUL SEARCH: Do I allow sinful things to pass before my eyes, or do I turn a blind eye to them?

**Father, put the fear of God between
my eyes and sin. Amen.**

October 24

PAST FINDING

Judgments are prepared for scoffers,
and beatings for the backs of fools.
—PROVERBS 19:29

It's wise to keep our mouth shut when it comes to the judgments of God. We tend to look on the outward and say that a certain person, or a certain city or group of people, will certainly be judged this side of judgment day.

But the truth is that the judgments of God are past finding. There are certain cities that are filled with people who we know live lifestyles that are an abomination to God, and yet those cities prosper. Then there are cities that are filled with professing Christians who have flooding destroy thousands of homes and take human lives. Other cities experience droughts and fires that also destroy and kill. Are these God's judgments on those cities? He alone knows.

The best we can say, and perhaps the only thing we should say, is that these are not signs of His favor, and sinners in all cities need to repent and trust the Savior, whether they are in prosperity or not.

SOUL SEARCH: How do I feel when I see these situations happening? Does it worry me that I don't understand the ways of God?

Father, help me to trust you with all my heart and not rely on my own understanding (Proverbs 3:5). Amen.

ROTTEN FRUIT

Wine is a mocker, strong drink is a brawler,
and whoever is led astray by it is not wise.

—PROVERBS 20:1

One of the greatest tragedies in the history of the human race was the day that man discovered that he could drain the poison from rotten fruit, drink it, and get rid of his inhibitions. The upside of the poison of alcohol was that it made him feel better; the downside was that it stirred his anger, impaired his judgments, caused addiction, and dulled his conscience.

And so we have wives who are beaten by angry drunken husbands, marriages destroyed, slaughter on our roads because of toxin-soaked drivers, and a massive trail of destruction, all because of alcoholism. Wine is certainly a mocker. It makes a pathetic slave out of those who are deceived by it. They are wise who don't let the poison of alcohol ever touch their lips.

SOUL SEARCH: What are my thoughts about alcohol? Have I ever been tempted to lean on it to cope?

**Father, never let me be deceived by the
lie of alcohol. Amen.**

THE SOUL

The wrath of a king is like the roaring of a lion;
whoever provokes him to anger sins against his own life.

—PROVERBS 20:2

*S*cripture warns that when a man joins himself to a prostitute, he sins against his own body (1 Corinthians 6:18). But if we anger God, we sin against our own soul. This is because the soul is eternal. Jesus warned that God should be feared because He can cast both body and soul into hell (Matthew 10:28).

The body radically changes over a lifetime. We sprout in our youth, bear fruit in our prime, and then wither and die in our old age. But the soul remains the same, except that it gathers experience and knowledge. It is eternal, and it's what leaves the body at death and faces God.

If we should fear an earthly king, how much more should we fear the heavenly King who presides over all! We have provoked His anger by our sins, but the roar of the lion of wrath will shut its mouth if we repent and trust the Savior. Its cry for justice is satisfied in Jesus Christ.

SOUL SEARCH: What do I care about—my body or my soul? Is this evident in my actions?

**Father, thank you that you are the lover
of my soul. Amen.**

October 27

LOVE AND GENTLENESS

It is honorable for a man to stop striving,
since any fool can start a quarrel.
—PROVERBS 20:3

*W*hen I was a child in school, I was often bullied by the bigger kids. But I learned at a young age the truth of this verse. If a bully twisted my arm up my back, I didn't play tough. Instead, I yelled before it hurt. That was wise because bullies tend to twist a little more before they let go.

As Christians it's sometimes easy to get into strife when sharing the gospel. We have an offensive message when it's shared in full. The key is to explain the hard-to-hear truths in love and gentleness. Those godly virtues tend to defuse strife. If someone does get angry when they hear us talk about sin, righteousness, and judgment, it's best to back off.

The Scriptures then say "any fool can start a quarrel," and we see that happen often in professional sports. If someone gets into one-on-one strife, in rush the fools like flies, who then turn it into a brawl.

It's best to once again learn from the Word of God and save ourselves some pain.

SOUL SEARCH: What tone do I use when sharing the gospel with others? Is my love for them evident?

Father, let love be my motivation for all that I do.
Amen.

COZY CHRISTENDOM

The lazy man will not plow because of winter;
he will beg during harvest and have nothing.
—PROVERBS 20:4

*T*he waters of evangelism are as cold as ice. So, understandably, most of us prefer to stay by the warm fire of cozy Christendom. It's there that we can discuss theology, theophany, geology, sanctification, evolution, infusion, importation, justification, and the amazing ramifications of the incarnation. Anything but do as we have been commanded to do—preach the gospel to every creature. For much of the busy modern church, it's as though hell doesn't exist.

If I was told to jump twenty feet from a bank down into icy waters, I would be paralyzed with fear. But if a four-year-old child had just fallen into the freezing water and was drowning, I would jump without fear or hesitation. Most of us would.

If we profess to have the love of God dwelling in us, we must ignore our fears and take the leap. Precious human lives are at stake.

SOUL SEARCH: Would I jump into icy water to save a drowning child? How does this compare to my willingness to save lives by sharing the gospel?

**Father, give me a love that will swallow my fears.
Amen.**

October 29

SELF-SUFFICIENCY

Counsel in the heart of man is like deep water,
but a man of understanding will draw it out.

—PROVERBS 20:5

It's a subtle pride that doesn't seek counsel. Self-sufficiency is often evidence of intellectual bankruptcy. Those who are wise in their own eyes are fools, and those who are fools in their own eyes are wise, because they will take the time to draw counsel from others. It is a wise youth who listens to those who are older. Those who do so can gain without the pain.

The Bible is a deep-watered ocean of wisdom from the heart of God. Those with understanding will draw out of it daily. The more we learn about life, the more we learn about how little we know. It's the knowledge that we lack that causes us to search the Scriptures, draw out truth, and hide it in our hearts.

SOUL SEARCH: Where does my sufficiency come from? Is it from myself or from God?

◦⟋◦

**Father, help me to rely on you for all things.
Amen.**

THE GOODNESS OF MAN

Most men will proclaim each his own goodness,
but who can find a faithful man?
—PROVERBS 20:6

*W*hile some may deny the truth of Scripture, no one could argue that this verse isn't true. Almost every human being thinks that they are morally good. If you don't believe it, ask someone, "Would you consider yourself to be a good person?" You will hear, "Yes, I think so," or "Absolutely!"

That question is a probe of the scalpel to see if surgery is necessary. If there is self-righteousness present, the patient needs a life-saving operation. He needs the law to bring the knowledge of sin.

This is what Jesus did in Mark 10:17. The rich young ruler had no understanding as to the definition of "good," so Jesus showed him God's standard by going through five of the Ten Commandments. We need to do the same to prepare sinners' hearts for the message of the cross.

SOUL SEARCH: Do I believe the testimony of the Bible fully or just in part? Does my life prove this?

Father, help me to have the courage to gently
confront sinners about their state before you. Amen.

HYPOCRISY

The righteous man walks in his integrity;
his children are blessed after him.
—PROVERBS 20:7

Nothing dissipates respect in children like hypocrisy in their parents. Children are not fooled by parents who lack integrity. They're watching to see if what they hear the preacher say on Sunday translates into the other six days of the week.

Do they see a husband who honors his wife, or do they see fighting between them? Does their father teach his children the Word of God, pray with them, and train them up in the way they should go? Or is he too busy to care about the eternal salvation of his children? Is their father honest, temperate, and God fearing?

If he is, then his children will be blessed after him. He will reproduce his own kind and have children who are honest, temperate, and God fearing.

SOUL SEARCH: When was the last time I embraced a double standard?

**Father, keep me free from hypocrisy.
Amen.**

November

THE COMPLEX EYE

A king who sits on the throne of judgment
scatters all evil with his eyes.

—PROVERBS 20:8

*T*he human eye is an unspeakably complex marvel that we rarely give a second thought. But in reality, it is a reflection of the utter genius of God. How could He make such a thing? How does His hand fashion an eye, let alone a matching pair that can see and communicate images to the brain? The eye has 137 million light-sensitive cells, and focusing muscles that move an estimated one hundred thousand times a day. Modern science has discovered that the instructions for how each eye was to be made was in our DNA from the moment we were conceived.[*]

Our eyes are also windows of the soul. They can instantly change to express joy, fear, evil, kindness, love, and pain, and with the right look we can even scatter all evil. Such thoughts are too high for us to comprehend, and no words can express worthy praise to God for His wonderful works.

SOUL SEARCH: When was the last time I was brought to a silent worship as I mediated on the power of God?

୬

**Father, I am awestruck by the greatness of your power,
and humbled by your love. Amen.**

---

[*] "Rod," *Encyclopædia Britannica*, https://www.britannica.com/science/rod
-retinal-cell; "40 Astounding Facts You Should Know About Your Amazing
Human Body," Distractify, http://distractify.com/old-school/2014
/07/20/amazing-facts-about-the-human-body-1197776387.

November 2

A CLEAN HEART

Who can say, "I have made my heart clean,
I am pure from my sin"?
—PROVERBS 20:9

*W*ho would want to say, "I have made my heart clean,
I am pure from my sin"? A hungry dog would rather part with a T-bone steak than an unregenerate man part with his sin. The Scriptures say that we love the darkness (John 3:19), and drink iniquity like a thirsty man drinks water (Job 15:16).

Before my conversion, I had no desire to divorce my sin—until I understood that sin and death are married to one another. We cannot have sin without death. So the irrelevant question as to how I could be free from sin became the most relevant question I ever asked.

Thank God it was answered in the mercy of God that was extended through Jesus Christ. He poured out his life's blood on the cross so that my heart could be clean and I could be pure from my sin on the great day of His wrath.

Such thoughts produce incredible gratitude, and at the same time a deep concern for those who have no care for their eternal salvation.

SOUL SEARCH: Do I hate even the temptation to sin, or do I tend to see some sins as more permissible?

*Father, may the only thirst I have be for you.
Amen.*

THE BEST POLICY

Diverse weights and diverse measures,
they are both alike, an abomination to the LORD.
—PROVERBS 20:10

We often hear maxims such as "honesty is the best policy." It probably comes from George Washington's "I hold the maxim no less applicable to public than to private affairs, that honesty is the best policy."* But we should be honest, not because it's best, or pays dividends, but because honesty is right.

Mark Twain said, "Every man is wholly honest to himself and to God, but not to anyone else."† He probably meant that only we and God know when we are being truly honest. Conversely, we both know when we cheat another person. The problem is that most of the time, only God sees it as an abomination.

May God so work in our hearts that when we even consider lying to or stealing from any other person, we also see it as an abomination.

SOUL SEARCH: Am I honest in all things before God and men, or do I tend to think it's okay to "stretch the truth"?

✶

**Father, may I be aware of your holiness and hatred
of even the smallest of sins. Amen.**

---

* "George Washington Quotes," George Washington's Mount Vernon, http://www.mountvernon.org/george-washington/quotes/article/i-hold-the-maxim-no-less-applicable-to-public-than-to-private-affairs-that-honesty-is-the-best-policy/.
† Caroline Thomas Harnsberger, ed., *Mark Twain at Your Fingertips: A Book of Quotations* (Mineola, NY: Dover Publications, Inc.), 180.

WILLFULLY BLIND

Even a child is known by his deeds,
whether what he does is pure or right.

—PROVERBS 20:11

Those who deny the existence of sin have either never had children or they are willfully blind.

If we care about our children, we will be continually telling them not to do wrong, and teaching them to do that which it right. They naturally know how to be selfish and ungrateful, and so it's normal for a child who is left without instruction to think that he is the center of the universe.

The key to good parenting is to believe the Bible when it says that human beings go astray from the womb, and to begin correction from the moment the child begins to demand his own way. If you are able to teach him to be unselfish and grateful to God, he will bring joy to your heart as he matures into his teenage years. But he will bring grief to his parents if he is left without instruction as to what is right and wrong, and if he's not taught to respect all authority.

SOUL SEARCH: What do my deeds say about me? Am I ready to do good today?

∽

**Father, please give me opportunities to show
your love in a practical way. Amen.**

THE EYE AND EAR

The hearing ear and the seeing eye,
the LORD has made them both.
—PROVERBS 20:12

Who would have believed that this verse would be applicable to any generation? It seems to be nothing but an example of superfluity. But perhaps it was written for such a time as this. We live among a generation of foolish people who think they're wise when they believe that the hearing ear made itself from nothing.

Notice that this isn't just an ear, but a "hearing" ear. How foolish it is to believe that what human beings can't make, made itself. The same applies to the "seeing" eye. How could anyone ever begin to make a seeing eye? Yet there are many unthinking people who believe the seeing eye made itself from nothing. Atheism is the epitome of unscientific lunacy.

May God help us to reach this blind generation before it's too late.

SOUL SEARCH: Am I unprepared and intimidated to speak to someone about atheism? If so, what steps can I take to overcome this?

⌒

Father, help me to be free of any intimidation that would hinder me from sharing the gospel. Amen.

A GOOD NIGHT'S SLEEP

Do not love sleep, lest you come to poverty; open your eyes,
and you shall be satisfied with bread.

—PROVERBS 20:13

While it's great to get a good night's sleep, it is an annoying addiction for those who value every waking moment of life. Even though the experience of sleeping can be pleasurable, we spend a third of our life in the unconscious state, often unwillingly being pulled into a realm of insanity.

Some dreams are wonderful, but most make little or no sense. We float across the sky on the back of an elephant along with a schoolteacher we haven't seen for years, drinking coffee from two-foot-tall cups. And it all makes sense, until we awaken. Then add to that the facts that most mornings we wake up feeling and looking as though we have been hit by a truck, and sleep rarely delivers what it seems to promise.

So don't ever have an inordinate love for sleep. Rather, open your eyes to the lost world, then take them the Bread of Life before they sleep in what the Bible calls "the sleep of death" (Psalm 13:3).

SOUL SEARCH: What can I do to make the best use of my waking hours?

⌒

Father, teach me to number my days, that I might
apply my heart to wisdom (Psalm 90:12). Amen.

THE BLINDED MIND

"It is good for nothing," cries the buyer;
but when he has gone his way, then he boasts.
—PROVERBS 20:14

he devil would have the world believe that life is worth-less—that people are nothing but stardust, the random result of a cosmic explosion caused by nothing. He would have them think that they have no meaning and no purpose. The father of lies feeds nothing but falsehoods to those who are taken captive to do his will. He blinds the minds of those whom he came to kill, steal from, and destroy (John 10:10). And he says of the gospel, "It is good for nothing."

But we know that the Good Shepherd came to save sinners. He came to rescue those who were appointed to die. He saved us not only from the devil, but also from death and hell.

Now we make our boasts in the Lord. We once thought the gospel was nothing and not worthy of a moment of thought, but now we sing of the mercy of God in Christ and will "boast in the Lord" (1 Corinthians 1:31 NIV) throughout eternity.

SOUL SEARCH: What are some of my boasts in the Lord? Is He my joy and crowned King?

**Father, give me opportunity to boast of you.
Amen.**

THE WHITENESS OF WHITE

There is gold and a multitude of rubies,
but the lips of knowledge are a precious jewel.

—PROVERBS 20:15

*C*omparisons give us contrast and therefore a perspective. We can best see how the color white is when it's compared to black, or how crooked a line is when it's compared to something that is straight. And we can see how precious knowledge is when it's compared to gold or a mountain of rubies.

But gold and rubies only have worth in this life, while the lips of knowledge kiss the edges of eternity. They have the power to overcome death. "If you confess with your mouth Jesus as Lord, and believe in your heart that God raised Him from the dead, you will be saved" (Romans 10:9).

But the lips of the Christian are perhaps most precious when they disperse the knowledge of salvation to a dying world.

SOUL SEARCH: What does my eternal salvation rest on? Am I trusting alone in Jesus without works for it?

Father, help me to share the knowledge of salvation with those who are still trapped by the power of death. Amen.

TRAPPED BY DEBT

Take the garment of one who is surety for a stranger,
and hold it as a pledge when it is for a seductress.

—PROVERBS 20:16

*I*n these times of mass media, it's tempting to live beyond our means. We can easily be tempted by clever advertisers who tell us that we need to buy their product. They bank on the greedy hearts of humanity, preying on the covetous, then the covetous borrow to get what they think they want and find themselves trapped by debt.

And so those sinking in debt find themselves reaching out to those who will pledge payment to their debtors. But the problem is deeper than just debt. It is the heart that needs changing, so that we're content.

It is not uncommon for those on government assistance to arrive in a taxi or to be clutching an expensive cell phone when they pick up their government check. So don't be a guarantor for the debt of a stranger. Reserve that rather for those you know.

SOUL SEARCH: Am I appreciative of the blessings I have today, or do I always yearn for more?

ᢏᡐ

**Father, may I trust you and give thanks for all things,
good or bad. Amen.**

MODERN ENTERTAINMENT

Bread gained by deceit is sweet to a man;
but afterward his mouth will be filled with gravel.

—PROVERBS 20:17

The Bible says that unregenerate human beings enjoy darkness (John 3:19). We don't merely like sin; we love it. We get pleasure out of evil.

The entertainment industry caters to this. What we watch simply reflects these desires, and so modern entertainment is filled with violence, adultery, fornication, blasphemy, homosexuality, lying, and stealing. But there is an unchanging law of sowing and reaping: Whatever we sow, that we will also reap. Sin may sow pleasure, but it eventually reaps pain.

What is sown into society creates a society filled with violence, adultery, fornication, homosexuality, blasphemy, lying, and stealing. That which was once entertaining now becomes reality. But the full harvest of what's been sown won't be seen until eternity.

SOUL SEARCH: What kind of things do I love? Are they lovely, pure, and of good report?

Father, may I ever be mindful of what
I sow into my soul. Amen.

GOOD ADVICE

Plans are established by counsel;
by wise counsel wage war.
—PROVERBS 20:18

*G*ood advice, when it comes to war, is that it should be avoided at all costs, if possible. It was necessary to stop Adolf Hitler in World War II, but that war cost fifty million lives. And we are told that most who died in that war were burned to death. War is nothing but a massive human tragedy, because it is so often the innocent who are caught in the crossfire.

As Christians, we know that there is a war going on between God and man, and that there are spiritual powers in high places (Ephesians 6:12) whose mission is "to steal, and to kill, and to destroy" (John 10:10). That is the war we should be primarily involved with—seeking above all things to snatch human lives from the hands of a very real and sinister enemy. That's good advice.

SOUL SEARCH: Am I aware that the enemy can influence my thoughts? How can I turn a deaf ear to him?

∽

Father, remind me to keep on the "helmet of salvation" (Ephesians 6:17) and to guard my thoughts (Proverbs 4:23). Amen.

November 12

EVANGELISTIC TALEBEARERS

He who goes about as a talebearer reveals secrets;
therefore do not associate with one who flatters with his lips.

—PROVERBS 20:19

Those who gossip "go about." They become evangelistic in their zeal to spread their interesting news, searching for someone who will listen to their succulent secrets.

Talebearers will often speak well of the person whose reputation they are about to destroy: "I really like so-and-so, but did you hear what someone said he did?" As much as we relish a tale, if we fear God, we will lend neither our lips nor our ears to the devil.

Neither meddle with a flatterer. Stay away from those who are prone to flatter or to gossip, in case you learn their ways. And keep in mind that it is often said that the person who will gossip to you, will gossip about you.

SOUL SEARCH: Do I engage in gossip, or do I avoid those who cause division?

Father, let me be a person who goes about with the gospel rather than with gossip. Amen.

DRUNKEN YOUTHS

Whoever curses his father or his mother,
his lamp will be put out in deep darkness.

—PROVERBS 20:20

*A*theists often point to the Bible as barbaric, because Hebrew civil law prescribed the death sentence for a youth who was continually a drunkard and was rebellious (Deuteronomy 21:18–21). While there is no recorded incident of that actually happening in Scripture, we must remember that that same harsh law will judge humanity on judgment day. Jesus said on that day, it will "grind … to powder" (Matthew 21:44).

When something is ground to powder, a thorough job is done. God will judge murderers, rapists, thieves, liars, adulterers, and fornicators. But he will also judge hatred, idle words, lust, and those who have cursed their parents.

We have to face a morally perfect God and a perfect law that will see that perfect justice is done. Every skeleton in the closet, every hidden motive, every deed done in darkness will be brought into the light (Ecclesiastes 12:14). That's why we must warn everyone, that we might present every man (and woman) perfect in Christ Jesus.

SOUL SEARCH: Do I confess my sins the moment I'm aware of them, or do I overlook them?

*Father, may I forever keep my lamp filled with oil
and brightly shining. Amen.*

OUR INHERITANCE

An inheritance gained hastily at the beginning
will not be blessed at the end.

—PROVERBS 20:21

We have an inheritance that God predestined before the foundation of the world. It was not gotten hastily.

I wonder how many unbelievers would cast aside a letter from a lawyer that said that they had an inheritance waiting for them? Most would at least look into the matter. Yet millions don't bother to even inquire as to what Jesus left in His will and testament—the New Testament.

Our inheritance is undefiled, reserved in heaven for those who are kept by faith until the day of our salvation. We await a new heaven and a new earth, and new bodies with no more pain, suffering, or death.

Oh, what a day that will be! How we long for it to come quickly, but at the same time we long for the multitudes of unsaved to come to the knowledge of God before it comes.

SOUL SEARCH: What am I more inclined to do—long for the coming kingdom or for more time?

**Father, may I rejoice because my name
is written in heaven. Amen.**

November 15

EVIL FOR EVIL

Do not say, "I will recompense evil"; wait for the LORD,
and He will save you.

—PROVERBS 20:22

It's human nature to want to pay back evil for evil, and the world will give you a hundred reasons why you should. But you shouldn't.

David was called "a man after [God's] own heart," and it was perhaps because (despite all his sins) he was a man of mercy. He didn't render evil for evil.

The world messes up the Scriptures in many ways. One of them is with an "eye for [an] eye" (Deuteronomy 19:21). They don't realize that it is a statute in God's law. If someone steals your ox, they are to pay back an ox—an eye for an eye, a tooth for a tooth. Nowadays we call it "restitution." But in personal dealings, we should never take the law into our own hands. Rather we let the courts deal out justice.

However, if the Christian is wronged, the high road for us is to give the problem to God and let Him deal with it for us.

SOUL SEARCH: When was the last time I was tempted to (or did) take the law into my own hands? What was the result?

Father, help me to be more like Jesus. Amen.

A TINY WEIGHT

Diverse weights are an abomination to the LORD;
and dishonest scales are not good.

—PROVERBS 20:23

*J*ust thirteen verses earlier in Proverbs, almost the identical words are said. Stealing is an abomination to God, even if it's done without the knowledge of the victim. A tiny weight isn't noticeable with one sale, but it is still theft, and thieves (even if they are petty thieves) will not inherit the kingdom of God.

Surely such warnings need to be repeated to the dull of healing. If such truth repeated a thousand times and a blind sinner repents after hearing it a thousand times, it is worth our time and effort. We must continue to repeat that each of us has been "weighed in the balances, and found wanting" (Daniel 5:7). And each of us is "wanting" a just wrath. Justice hovers over us like a massive gavel, until we come to the Savior and He stills its holy hand.

SOUL SEARCH: Do I steal small things and excuse myself because of the low value of the stolen item? If so, how does God feel about this?

Father, shame me if I ever steal. Amen.

ORDERED STEPS

A man's steps are of the Lord;
how then can a man understand his own way?

—PROVERBS 20:24

The psalmist said, "O Lord, You have searched me and known me. You know my sitting down and my rising up; You understand my thought afar off. You comprehend my path and my lying down, and are acquainted with all my ways. For there is not a word on my tongue, but behold, O Lord, You know it altogether. You have hedged me behind and before, and laid Your hand upon me. Such knowledge is too wonderful for me; it is high; I cannot attain it" (Psalm 139:1–6).

We may think we choose our paths, but God intervenes and directs. He orders the steps of the godly (Psalm 37:23). He causes people and circumstances to cross our paths, and when we look back at our lives, we can see His faithful hand in all we have done. For the godly, such thoughts are wonderful beyond words.

He cares for the lowly sparrow (Matthew 10:29). So how much more will He care for those whom He has redeemed by His blood! This is beyond our understanding, but it is a source of great joy.

SOUL SEARCH: When was the last time I thanked God for His providence?

**Father, thank you for your loving care this day.
Amen.**

OUR INSTRUCTIONS

It is a snare for a man to devote rashly something as holy,
and afterward to reconsider his vows.

—PROVERBS 20:25

Skeptics often point to terrible violence or sinful sexual behavior in the Bible. They will say that Lot offered his daughters to homosexuals in Sodom, as if the Bible is saying it was the right thing to do. But what they don't seem to know is that the Scriptures were written for our instruction. What Lot did was wrong, and it was stupid. Lesson there.

A classic example of a rash vow was Jephthah's promise to sacrifice to the Lord whatever came out of his house to meet him on his return from a battle (Judges 11:30–35). That was also really stupid; it was an example of what not to do.

It's best not to make any vows to God. Don't offer Him something if He will do something for you. Instead, keep your lips together and trust Him with your future, and whatever happens, you have His promise that it will be for your good. He knows what's best for us.

SOUL SEARCH: What is one mistake that I've learned from? Am I instructed by the mistakes of others?

⌁

**Father, instruct and guide me, in your
great faithfulness. Amen.**

THE DAY IS COMING

A wise king sifts out the wicked,
and brings the threshing wheel over them.

—PROVERBS 20:26

*T*he threshing wheel is what separates the wheat from the chaff. It's a sad day when any nation fails to turn the wheels of justice. It is a tragedy for the people when civil law loses the power to deter crime. When retribution is no longer feared, a nation will be given to crime.

The human heart is so wicked that the conscience is not enough to hold it back from serious criminal activity. When someone commits murder, he often thinks that he will get away with it. Add to that the thought that even if he gets caught, he will probably only get a few years in prison, and then there is little to stop him. This is why the law needs to have teeth enough for us to fear the consequences of its violation.

Whatever the case, the day will come when ultimate justice will be done. On judgment day, God will bring the wheel over the wicked, and Jesus warned that it will grind to powder.

SOUL SEARCH: What am I seeking this day with my actions? Do I hope for God's favor or the favor of others?

Father, help me to be eternally minded
as I go about this day. Amen.

THE MACHINE

The spirit of a man is the lamp of the LORD,
searching all the inner depths of the heart.
—PROVERBS 20:27

It's been said that your body is the machine in which you live, while the soul is the real you—your self-conscious part. But your spirit is your God-conscious part.

In our unregenerate state, our spirit is dead in sin (we are not conscious of the presence of God), but from the moment we are born again, our spirit comes alive and we become conscious of His immediate presence. The spirit is the lamp of the Lord. He lights up our life, and takes us out of darkness into the glorious light.

The "heart" is the very essence of each of us. Jesus said, "He who believes in Me, as the Scripture has said, out of his heart will flow rivers of living water" (John 7:38). That's the reason God gave us His Holy Spirit. He gives us the power to take living water to those who are dying without the Savior. Let it flow today.

SOUL SEARCH: In what ways do I act as a vessel that flows with living water?

**Father, make me a vessel of your precious
Holy Spirit today. Amen.**

UPHELD BY MERCY

Mercy and truth preserve the king;
and by lovingkindness he upholds his throne.
—PROVERBS 20:28

The Scriptures tell us that the law came by Moses, but grace and truth came by Jesus Christ (John 1:17). The law condemned us, but God extended His mercy through the gospel. God's throne is upheld by lovingkindness, and it is because of that wonderful virtue of the divine nature that we are preserved in Jesus Christ.

After David committed adultery and murder, it was to that throne that he appealed. He cried, "Have mercy upon me, O God, according to Your lovingkindness; according to the multitude of Your tender mercies, blot out my transgressions" (Psalm 51:1). If it weren't for the everlasting multitude of the tender mercies of God, we wouldn't have a gospel to preach, but would rather be awaiting fearful judgment and damnation.

SOUL SEARCH: When was the last time I thanked God for His mercy? Do I trust in it daily?

Father, I am eternally grateful that your
"mercy endures forever" (Psalm 136:1). Amen.

November 22

GRAY HAIR

The glory of young men is their strength,
and the splendor of old men is their gray head.

—PROVERBS 20:29

*T*he strength and enthusiasm of youth, without knowledge that comes by experience, is a recipe for disaster. Samson certainly had strength, but he lacked the wisdom to use his strength rightly. He compromised with the enemy, and that was to the death of him.

If you are young, use your gray matter and listen to those with the gray hair. It's often difficult for the young to hear the voice of experience, because when we are young we think we know everything. We are like a climbing toddler who learns the reality of gravity with bruises and pain. But those with gray hair have often learned life's lessons because of bruising and pain, and their pain can be your gain, if you will listen.

SOUL SEARCH: What would be one example of when I had zeal without knowledge?

*Father, thank you that your terrible pain
was for my eternal gain. Amen.*

November 23

NO VISIBLE MEANS

Blows that hurt cleanse away evil,
as do stripes the inner depths of the heart.
—PROVERBS 20:30

*M*atthew Henry said of this verse, "Severe rebukes sometimes do a great deal of good. But such is the corruption of nature, that men are loth to be rebuked for their sins. If God uses severe afflictions, to purify our hearts and fit us for his service, we have cause to be very thankful."*

The psalmist said it was good for him that he was afflicted because it was then that he learned God's statutes (Psalm 119:71). Though we don't like to admit it, times of severe chastening bring us to knees, and that's the safest place to be for a Christian.

Our problem is that it's no fun to be in the lions' den or at the edge of the Red Sea, with no visible means of escape. But it's at the times of helplessness that we learn that there is never hopelessness. And so we don't look to the lions or the Red Sea. Instead we look to Him whose promises are "an anchor of the soul, both sure and steadfast" (Hebrews 6:19).

SOUL SEARCH: What affliction have I faced and then found that much good came from it?

⌒

**Father, thank you for the loving hand that
chastens me when I need it. Amen.**

---

* *Matthew Henry's Concise Commentary* (Proverbs 20:30), Christianity.com, http://www.christianity.com/bible/commentary.php?com=mh-c&b=20&c=20.

November 24

HIS PERMISSION

The king's heart is in the hand of the LORD,
like the rivers of water; He turns it wherever He wishes.
—PROVERBS 21:1

There is not a dog that barks, a flea that jumps, a bird that sings, or even a heart that beats, outside the permissive will of God. The Bible says that from Him and through Him and to Him are *all* things (Romans 11:36). Kings, presidents, and nations don't make one move without His allowance. All the nations before Him are as a drop in a bucket—less than nothing. And their opposition to His perfect will is less than nothing.

The esteemed leaders of the nations may make decisions that they thought were their own. But they are, in truth, God directives. For those who understand the character and nature of almighty God, such thoughts are wonderfully consoling. In this world of evil and chaos, God is completely in control.

SOUL SEARCH: When was a time when I felt like God let go of His control over my life? How did that situation play out?

**Father, I trust you despite my negative feelings.
Amen.**

DUMB SHEEP

Every way of a man is right in his own eyes,
but the LORD weighs the hearts.

—PROVERBS 21:2

*E*very man is right in his own eyes. Until we come to the Good Shepherd, we are all like dumb sheep that have turned every one to his own way. We are convinced that our way is right, when it's not. This is why we need God's law (including the Ten Commandments) to show us that the path we are on leads to destruction. The law gives us light; it shows us the danger.

Oh, how I thank God for the day that He used it to show me my terrible error. When I read the warnings of Jesus, that God saw my lust as adultery, it was like an arrow in my heart. The law called for my blood and sent me fleeing to Him who redeemed us from the curse of the law, being made a curse for us.

So never despise the law. It is the mirror that gives us a glimpse of our state before a holy God. Use it as such for others, who think that they are doing what is right but are heading for a very real hell. Hold up the mirror and plead with them to turn to the Savior while they still have time.

SOUL SEARCH: Which of God's laws have I despised?

✧

Father, I say with the psalmist that I love your law (Psalm 119:97), and with Paul that I delight in it (Romans 7:22). Amen.

BETTER THAN SACRIFICE

To do righteousness and judgment
is more acceptable to the Lᴏʀᴅ than sacrifice.
—PROVERBS 21:3

*M*y dog has yet to learn the principle that obedience is better than sacrifice. When I tell him to come to me, I don't want him to roll over. But he often does. That may not seem too important—until he's on the road with a truck coming.

It was King Saul who learned that lesson the hard way. He offered a sacrifice when he should have done what he was told to by Samuel, and he was rebuked (1 Samuel 13:1–15). Today, our churches are full of people who offer the sacrifice of praise each Sunday but then ignore obedience to the Great Commission for the rest of the week.

May we always be obedient, and encourage others within the church to remember that hell is real and that we need laborers who will harvest.

SOUL SEARCH: When was the last time I offered some sort of sacrifice to God rather than obeyed what I know is right?

**Father, help me to always have an obedient attitude.
Amen.**

WALK IN HIS STATUTES

A haughty look, a proud heart,
and the plowing of the wicked are sin.

—PROVERBS 21:4

The word (or the letter) *i* is right in the middle of *pride*, and it is our self-will that is the root of pride: "I will not bend the knee to God."

Psalm 10:4 says, "The wicked in his proud countenance does not seek God." It's not that he *cannot* find God, but that in his pride and arrogance, he *will not* seek Him. He chooses darkness rather than light, and to go his own way rather than humble himself before the God who gave him life.

However, when our sinful heart humbles itself before God, He makes His will ours. We find ourselves saying, "I delight to do Your will, O my God" (Psalm 40:8). Through the new birth of John 3:1–21, He causes us not only to walk in His statutes, but also to love to do so.

SOUL SEARCH: What is the posture of my heart? Is it contrite and humble?

◯

Father, today cause me to delight to please you.
Amen.

November 28

SELF-MADE PEOPLE

The plans of the diligent lead surely to plenty,
but those of everyone who is hasty, surely to poverty.
—PROVERBS 21:5

*I*f you speak to the rich, you will find that most who are self-made will tell you that they were diligent. They worked hard and it paid off. And more than likely, one key to their wealth is that they weren't hasty in their decisions.

However, if you are saved, having plenty will be secondary in your thoughts. You would rather have learned the virtue of contentment. Now your thoughts aren't fed by a desire to store up wealth, but that sinners would be saved from a very real hell.

This is what consumed the apostle Paul's thoughts. He was overwhelmed with a deep concern for the salvation of the lost, saying that we should strive to, by any and all means, save some. Then he told us to imitate him. May we do that today.

SOUL SEARCH: How often do I pray for the unsaved to come to the cross? Do I do it daily?

∽

**Father, please send revival to this sinful world
before death pulls them into eternity. Amen.**

PARTNER IN CRIME

Getting treasures by a lying tongue
is the fleeting fantasy of those who seek death.

—PROVERBS 21:6

Hananias and his partner in crime, Sapphira, lacked the fear of God. In lying to the Holy Spirit, they sought their own death (Acts 5:1–11). How foolish of them to think that they could fool God, and how foolish of us to ever think we could do the same.

Before we came to the foot of the cross, we had no idea that we were seeking death. But every time we sinned, we provoked the Great Reaper. The wrath of God hovered over us (John 3:36). Sin's wages were waiting to be paid out, and how we now thank God that He held back death's power until we were safe in Jesus.

The greatest favor we can do for ourselves is to cultivate the fear of the Lord. We do that by seeing our sins, seeing God's perfect holiness, and then seeing the contrast between the two. The difference should make us tremble. But if we can't tremble at our own sinfulness, we should tremble at the cost of our redemption.

SOUL SEARCH: When was the last time I truly considered what would have happened had the grace of God not entered my life?

*Father, keep me remembering your
great love for me. Amen.*

MAN AND BEASTS

The violence of the wicked will destroy them,
because they refuse to do justice.

—PROVERBS 21:7

The massive difference between humans and beasts is our moral understanding. We intuitively know right from wrong, and when we ignore that compass, we sin against God. No animal sets up court systems with judges and juries. This is evidence that we are unique in creation, and this uniqueness is there because we are made in the image of Him who is the habitation of justice.

The violence of the wicked—their lies, their lusts, and their rebellion against God—will come back to them in the form of a terrible eternal justice. God is storing up wrath with every transgression.

Let's pray that the wicked will hear the words of life in Jesus Christ, and trust alone in Him before the day of wrath, always keeping in mind the sobering truth of "There but for the grace of God go I."

SOUL SEARCH: Do I tend to glorify myself, or do I seek to glorify God?

**Father, may I glorify you today in my thoughts,
words, and deeds. Amen.**

December

FEARFUL PITFALLS

The way of a guilty man is perverse;
but as for the pure, his work is right.

—PROVERBS 21:8

The ungodly are like the lost sheep that have turned to their own way. Every one of them has gone astray. And so it is understandable when they fall into a ravine or are devoured by wolves.

Christians, however, know that life is filled with fearful pitfalls, and they're aware of them because God has opened the eyes of their understanding. They also know that deep pits are often surrounded by attractive flowers that beckon to be picked. When adultery, fornication, pornography, and other sensual sins beckon, they don't hear. This is because they have reckoned their sinful desires dead, and in doing so have rendered the wolf unable to harm them. Through their faith in the cleansing blood of the Savior, they are seen as pure, and their work is right in the eyes of holy God.

SOUL SEARCH: How do I view sin? Do I see it as a risky pleasure or a fearful pitfall?

Father, may I fear sin as I would hell.
Amen.

YOUTH CAMP BREAKFAST

Better to dwell in a corner of the housetop,
than in a house shared with a contentious woman.

—PROVERBS 21:9

I have often said that the best time a young man and young woman should consider each other for marriage is at breakfast on the second day of a Christian youth camp. This is because few have had any sleep by the second day, and at that time of the morning you are seeing what you are getting. The point being that it is so important to look for godly character, rather than superficial and fading looks, in a husband or wife. The engine of the vehicle is of more importance than the body.

Hollywood is mostly made up of selfish people who are of very shallow character. This is reflected in the high divorce rate. Instead of going to the corner of the housetop to think clearly, they go to the corner divorce lawyer. This would never happen in Christian circles if we began relationships by looking for godliness in the lives of those we wish to marry.

SOUL SEARCH: How would I define godly character?

*Father, make me so godly that others
may see you in me. Amen.*

YOUR FATHER

The soul of the wicked desires evil;
his neighbor finds no favor in his eyes.

—PROVERBS 21:10

It's telling to note that with just the addition of one letter, the word *evil* becomes *devil*. Even though most would consider themselves good people with perhaps a capacity to do evil, the devil is our father.

Jesus said of the religious leaders of His time that they were of their father, the devil (John 8:44). The best of us is evil through and through, and our hearts are "deceitful … and desperately wicked" (Jeremiah 17:9). And yet, therein is hidden the greatest consolation for the Christian: Christ died for us while we were in our evil state (Romans 5:8), showing that God's love for us is unconditional.

He loved us, not because we somehow merited it but because He is the reservoir of love and couldn't contain Himself. That means we needn't perform to be loved. We need to only believe that we are loved, and that the love He has for us is everlasting.

SOUL SEARCH: When I look at the cross, what do I see? Do I see God's love for me?

Father, may I understand your love expressed through
the cross, to a point that I need to look no further
for assurance of your love. Amen.

AN OPEN INVITATION

When the scoffer is punished,
the simple is made wise; but when the wise is instructed,
he receives knowledge.

—PROVERBS 21:11

There is no excuse for us if we lack wisdom. God has given each of us an open invitation to wisdom by saying that if anyone lacks wisdom, let him ask God and He will give it liberally (James 1:5). Each of us needs wisdom to navigate through the complexities of daily life. We need it in our marriages and in our jobs, and we need it to discern the subtlety of the enemy. We need it when we speak to the lost, when we pray, and when we read God's Word.

So plead with your Father for the precious jewel of wisdom, with an importunity of him who is desperate for an answer. You will find, in time, that you are making wise decisions and saying wise things, because your faithful Creator is true to His Word.

SOUL SEARCH: How often do I pray for wisdom?

**Father, make me wiser today than I was yesterday.
Amen.**

December 5

TWO BUILDERS

The righteous God wisely considers the house of the wicked,
overthrowing the wicked for their wickedness.
—PROVERBS 21:12

*A*ll of humanity is made up of two builders. The wise build their house on the foundation of the teachings of Jesus Christ. The foolish don't, and when the storms of life come, the wise remain standing while the foolish collapse (Matthew 7:24–27).

Notice that both the foolish and the wise have storms come their way. We can't avoid them. It is therefore wise to fortify ourselves with an unshakable trust in God. Have the attitude that *when* tragedy hits, you will trust Him no matter what.

Also consider those who are still in their sins, and what will happen when their storms come. Pity them, pray for them, preach to them, and plead with them to turn to the Savior before the ultimate storm hits.

SOUL SEARCH: What is the foundation of my life? Have I built upon the person of Jesus Christ?

Father, never let me build on anything outside of the teachings of your Word. Amen.

SOLVE THE DILEMMA

Whoever shuts his ears to the cry of the poor
will also cry himself and not be heard.

—PROVERBS 21:13

*T*he world often pities those who are less fortunate, but the Christian goes further, with empathy. Pity pities, but empathy does something about the problem. That's why you see so many homeless shelters, hospitals, and soup kitchens that are run by Christian organizations. We are told to "remember the poor" (Galatians 2:10).

That leaves many of us who want to help in a dilemma, as we exit freeways and see the homeless pleading for money. Do we give them cash, risking that they will use it for drugs, cigarettes, or alcohol? One way to solve this dilemma is to keep packages for the homeless in our vehicle, including things like health bars, toothpaste, water, a gift card, and a New Testament or gospel tract. Jesus said that there will always be poor people (Mark 14:7), but each of us can do a little to help them in their suffering.

SOUL SEARCH: When it comes to the misfortune of others, do I feel pity or empathy?

✐

Father, please give me your empathy. Amen.

PACIFYING ANGER

A gift in secret pacifies anger,
and a bribe behind the back, strong wrath.

—PROVERBS 21:14

This verse is a wonderful gem when it comes to reaching the lost. The message we preach sometimes angers the ungodly. When they're confronted with the moral law, it brings a sense of guilt, and sometimes sinners try to shed the guilt with anger.

We sometimes do this when we are in an argument and suddenly see that we're in the wrong. We can either humble ourselves and apologize, or we can get angry and leave by slamming a door. The latter allows us to keep our pride.

However, anger can be defused by a gift that expresses love for the person to whom you are witnessing. I almost always give someone a five-dollar gift card after I've witnessed to them, and say, "Thank you for listening to me. I really appreciate it." That small gift can speak louder than a thousand sermons.

SOUL SEARCH: How do I treat unsaved people? Am I kind and generous to them for the sake of the gospel?

Father, make me a giver of myself, my talents, and my resources. Amen.

December 8

SINGING MOUNTAINS

It is a joy for the just to do justice,
but destruction will come to the workers of iniquity.
—PROVERBS 21:15

*M*ovies that end with the bully getting his face rubbed in the mud are always winners at the box office.

As Christians we should hate any form of injustice, from bullying to mass murder. There have been cases where criminals have shot a police officer in the face simply because the officer was trying to protect society and do what is right. It's a huge consolation when such cruel criminals are brought to justice!

But when they get away with murder, it is truly grievous and makes us long for judgment day. On that day, perfect justice will be done. The Bible uses personification in describing it, saying that there will be such joy that even the mountains will break forth into singing (Isaiah 55:12).

SOUL SEARCH: How often do I pray for all those in authority, including the police?

*Father, help me to be an intercessor
for the leaders of my nation. Amen.*

THE NATURE OF GOD

The man who wanders from the way of understanding
will rest in the assembly of the dead.

—PROVERBS 21:16

We live among a generation that has wandered from the way of understanding. They are in the congregation of the dead, and will stay there without an understanding of the nature of God and the nature of sin.

When a nation loses the fear of the Lord, it turns to idolatry. And idolatry (making up your own image of God) has no moral dictate. A false god doesn't say that anything is morally wrong, and that opens the door to all sorts of sin. That is why the church (in the pulpits and the in the streets) needs to use the law of God to bring back a biblical understanding of both the character of our Creator and the nature of sin.

SOUL SEARCH: Do I represent the true nature of God as revealed by Scripture? If so, how? If not, what do I need to change so I will?

Father, may I never soften any of your attributes.
Amen.

PERSONAL HAPPINESS

He who loves pleasure will be a poor man:
he who loves wine and oil will not be rich.

—PROVERBS 21:17

The force that drives most human beings is a desire for personal pleasure. That's understandable. Each of us wants to be happy. However, the key to the direction of the driving force for the Christian is to always make righteousness our destination. In other words, we should make God's pleasure our pleasure.

The way to determine what it is that pleases God is to search His Word; and it tells us that He loves righteousness, justice, integrity, and truth. He also loved human beings enough to become one Himself and suffer and die on an unspeakably cruel cross.

If we are to please God, we should strive to love people enough to tell them how they can find everlasting life. When one sinner comes to a place of genuine repentance, Jesus said it causes heaven to rejoice (Luke 15:10), and heaven's pleasure should be our pleasure.

SOUL SEARCH: How do I feel about those who are difficult to love? Do I have deep care and compassion for them?

Father, may I never have a hard-hearted attitude toward any other human being. Amen.

DIFFICULT VERSES

The wicked shall be a ransom for the righteous,
and the unfaithful for the upright.

—PROVERBS 21:18

*E**llicott's Commentary for English Readers* says of this rather strange verse ("The wicked shall be a ransom for the righteous") that "the righteous is 'delivered out of trouble (Proverbs 11:8; comp. Isaiah 57:1), and the wicked cometh in his stead' to receive upon his own head God's descending punishment. So it was with Mordecai and Haman."*

The godly say of this and other hard-to-understand Bible verses, "This is God's Word. How would we ever understand it completely? If it doesn't make sense, it's only because we lack understanding." Such is the way of the humble. The God-fearing always justify God. In other words, they *always* say that God is right and we are always wrong.

In contrast, however, if there is any contention between the proud world and the Word of God, the world always justifies itself.

SOUL SEARCH: How do I handle hard-to-understand verses? Do I conquer them by trusting God?

Father, help me to trust your integrity. Amen.

---

* *Ellicott's Commentary for English Readers* (Proverbs 21:18), Biblehub.com, http://biblehub.com/commentaries/ellicott/proverbs/21.htm.

ANGRY WOMEN

Better to dwell in the wilderness,
than with a contentious and angry woman.
—PROVERBS 21:19

Not many of us like to be alone for too long. They say solitary confinement in a prison is torturous because we crave interaction with other human beings. This Scripture says that it's better to be alone in a wilderness than to be with a contentious and angry woman.

I know this to be true.

I was once beaten up by a very angry woman who didn't like what I had said. I was preaching in the open air when she cussed at me, so I asked her to watch her language because there were ladies present. When she said, "I'm a lady," I unwisely replied, "Madame, you may be a woman, but you're not a lady."

That's when she beat me up. It took two weeks for the bruising to go away.

SOUL SEARCH: Do I avoid contention, or do I run toward it? Why?

Father, make me wise with my words.
Amen.

OUR TREASURE

There is desirable treasure and oil in the dwelling of the wise;
but a foolish man squanders it.
—PROVERBS 21:20

*W*hat we treasure in this short life reveals our wisdom, or lack of it. The ungodly treasure wealth and power because those things promise happiness, and personal happiness is the high idea of this world.

However, the Christian has a treasure that is so valuable that the world would do anything to have what we have, if they knew we had it. We have what Scripture refers to as "treasure in earthen vessels" (2 Corinthians 4:7). The treasure we have found in Christ is the source of everlasting life. We have found immortality in Christ! Jesus has abolished death and brought life and immortality to light through the gospel. Paul called what we have "Christ in you, the hope of glory" (Colossians 1:27).

May God give us the wisdom to make known what we have in Christ.

SOUL SEARCH: How often do I think about what to say to the unsaved?

Father, teach me how to reach sinners
before it's too late. Amen.

December 14

THE GLORIOUS GOSPEL

He who follows righteousness and mercy finds life,
righteousness, and honor.
—PROVERBS 21:21

*H*erein is the glorious gospel. The law demands the perfect righteousness of a morally perfect Creator. It cannot be separated from God, because it issues from His character.

Most people aren't at all concerned that the law works wrath until they understand that God sees the thought life and desires "truth in the inward parts" (Psalm 51:6). He sees lust as adultery and hatred as murder, and every time we sin, we store up His wrath that will be made manifest on judgment day.

It is because of the righteousness of the law that we need the mercy of God in Christ. Such is the way to everlasting life. God honors those who are clothed in the righteousness of God in Christ.

SOUL SEARCH: What does God see when He looks at my "inward parts"? Do I believe that He honors my prayers in Christ?

*Father, thank you that you honor my prayers because
I stand in the perfect righteousness of your Son. Amen.*

THE LEVEL PLAYING FIELD

A wise man scales the city of the mighty,
and brings down the trusted stronghold.

—PROVERBS 21:22

*W*e have the wisdom from above—a wisdom that's not of this world—and the weapons we use are not carnal, but mighty through God, to the pulling down of strongholds. Therefore, we never need to feel intimidated by the ungodly.

When we share the gospel with someone who we know has a great intellect, we bring them down to a level playing field by going around their intellect and addressing the conscience with the moral law. This is the way to scale the walls they put between themselves and God. The law casts down the strength of their confidence and leaves them undone before a holy God. This is how they are able to see this danger and their desperate need of the Savior.

SOUL SEARCH: What type of people intimidate me into silence when it comes to sharing my faith? Would I have difficulty sharing with a celebrity, a famous politician, or a very wealthy businessman or businesswoman?

Father, help me never to be a respecter of persons. Amen.

FIRE NEEDS FUEL

Whoever guards his mouth and his tongue
keeps his soul from troubles.
—PROVERBS 21:23

ire needs fuel to survive. Don't feed the flames. Don't give your opinion. Keep it to yourself, or pray about it. Stay within the safety of your thoughts and you will be happier. This is because we all come from different experiences and therefore have different perspectives. Each of us thinks that we are right. About everything. Always. I know I'm right about this. Probably.

And so we clash. What we see as a smart opinion, somebody else sees as foolish interfering. What we see as a solution, someone else sees as none of our business. What we think will make something better often makes it worse.

Best to bite the lip. The world won't come to an end if you keep your lips sealed. Do that, and you will save yourself trouble. You have God's word on that.

SOUL SEARCH: When was the last time my mouth got me into trouble? What did I learn from that?

ᴐ

**Father, give me the wisdom to speak when I ought,
and not to when it will get me into trouble. Amen.**

ARROGANT BIRDS

A proud and haughty man—"Scoffer" is his name;
he acts with arrogant pride.
—PROVERBS 21:24

*P*roud peacocks puff their feathers to make themselves look bigger than they are. So is every proud peacock who puffs himself up and rails against the godly. These arrogant birds make out that they're more intelligent than those who believe the childish stories of the Bible. But the Scriptures tell us that God has chosen foolish things to confound those who are wise (1 Corinthians 1:27). He resists the proud peacock and gives grace to the humble sparrow.

The Scriptures say, "Blessed is the man ... [who] sits [not] in the seat of the scornful" (Psalm 1:1). We are blessed if we don't join in their scorning, because scorn is rooted in pride. God gives grace only to the humble, and it is by His grace alone that we find everlasting life. For this reason, the scorner is to be pitied—because of where his scorn will take him.

SOUL SEARCH: How patient am I with scoffers?

**Father, give me the patience of Job and
the meekness of Moses. Amen.**

FUELED BY DESIRE

The desire of the lazy man kills him,
for his hands refuse to labor.
—PROVERBS 21:25

*E*very good work in this life begins with a thought, is fueled by desire, and is accomplished with sweat and muscle. Ships have been launched, books written, movies produced, planes flown, and buildings constructed—and every one of these endeavors has begun with the seed of desire.

The lazy person has the thought that produces the desire, but he shuns making it into a reality. It comes to nothing.

Little in this life that is worthwhile is served to us on a golden plate. We have to work for it, but with that work comes a sense of accomplishment.

The Bible calls evangelism a "labor." We sow in tears but will reap with joy (Psalm 126:5). Jesus said that the laborers of His time were few (Luke 10:2). They still are. Are you a laborer in the gospel? Have you had that thought spark a desire? Then make it happen today, and as you lay your head on your pillow tonight, you will have a sense of accomplishment that you have labored for your Lord.

SOUL SEARCH: When was the last time I put desire into action when it comes to reaching the lost?

⁓

**Father, may I pass from this life knowing that
I have been a good and faithful servant. Amen.**

GREED ISN'T GOOD

He covets greedily all the day long,
but the righteous gives and does not spare.
—PROVERBS 21:26

In the 1987 movie *Wall Street*, actor Michael Douglas made a speech that epitomized this world's ethics. He said, "The point is, ladies and gentleman, that greed—for lack of a better word—is good. Greed is right. Greed works. Greed clarifies, cuts through, and captures the essence of the evolutionary spirit. Greed, in all of its forms—greed for life, for money, for love, knowledge—has marked the upward surge of mankind."* These words are revealing. Darwinian evolution is a vain attempt to try to rid ourselves of the moral law, because it (among other things) encourages greed.

Greed is not good. It destroys families, and it has marked the downward surge of humankind. Guard against covetousness, greed, and ambition by having a financially generous spirit.

SOUL SEARCH: How do I feel about gambling and winning large amounts of money? Have I ever wished to do either?

Father, keep me from the sin of greed. Amen.

---

* "Wall Street Quotes," IMDb.com, http://www.imdb.com/title/tt0094291/quotes.

GOOD WORKS,
NO GOD

The sacrifice of the wicked is an abomination;
how much more when he brings it with wicked intent!

—PROVERBS 21:27

The basis of all the great religions is something that is commonly called "works righteousness." The ungodly think that they can make some sort of sacrifice, either with religious or "good" works, to please God.

The belief that separates Christianity from these religions is the moral law. It shows us the nature of sin and leaves us all as guilty criminals before the judgment bar of a holy God. The law shows that our "good" works are nothing but an attempt to bribe the Judge of the universe, and God will not be bribed. No amount of good works will turn His face away from the sin.

In Christianity, God provided the payment Himself, in the form of the cross of Calvary. The only thing that can now save us is the mercy of the Judge, and that's what we have in the gospel of Jesus Christ.

SOUL SEARCH: How often do I pray for the millions who are religious and yet hopeless in their quest for immortality?

Father, I cry out for your mercy to be extended
to those who are seeking salvation. Amen.

December 21

EARS TO HEAR

A false witness shall perish,
but the man who hears him will speak endlessly.
—PROVERBS 21:28

The Scriptures refer to Jesus as "the Faithful and True Witness" (Revelation 3:14). May we be the same—both faithful and true. Too many who call themselves Christians today are not true and faithful to preach about sin, and to warn the wicked of the reality of hell.

However, those who fear God will say with the apostle Paul, "Knowing, therefore, the terror of the Lord, we persuade men" (2 Corinthians 5:11). Few people nowadays know the terror of the Lord. The image they have of our Creator is one of a benevolent father figure, with no sense of justice or righteousness.

Jesus said, "He who has ears to hear, let him hear!" (Matthew 11:15). If we have heard the thunderings of God's law, and if we've seen the blood of the cross of Jesus Christ, we will tremble and say with the apostles, "We cannot but speak the things which we have heard and seen" (Acts 4:20).

SOUL SEARCH: What do I experience when I think of my sinful desires? Do I tremble at the thought of them?

᠅

**Father, may I say that I cannot but speak of that
which I have seen and heard. Amen.**

SHEEP AND GOATS

A wicked man hardens his face,
but as for the upright, he establishes his way.
—PROVERBS 21:29

Sheep and goats have some interesting differences. The main one is that goats are stubborn; they are not easily led like sheep. Goats are naturally independent, while sheep have an instinct to gather together in a flock.

The Bible likens false converts to goats. They secretly hold on to their own rebellious will. They call Jesus "Lord" but refuse to do the things He tells them to do.

The parable of the sower makes it clear that the true church is made up of true and false converts. Jesus referred to the false as goats amid the sheep, tares among the wheat, bad fish among the good, and foolish virgins among the wise, and said that they will be separated on the day of judgment (see Matthew 7:21–23). It is therefore wise for each of us to "examine" ourselves to see if we are "in the faith" (2 Corinthians 13:5). Do we harden our face to the voice of the Good Shepherd, or do we direct our way in obedience to His every word?

SOUL SEARCH: Am I a sheep or a goat? Why?

**Father, make me one who hears your voice
and follows you. Amen.**

THOMAS EDISON

There is no wisdom or understanding
or counsel against the LORD.

—PROVERBS 21:30

*I*f I had a worldly hero, it would be Thomas Edison. Atheists claim he was one of them, but he wasn't. He claimed to believe in the existence of a Supreme Intelligence pervading the universe. He was ungodly, but he was no fool.

Not only was he the ultimate inventor, but he also wasn't afraid of failure. He said that failure taught him what not to do. But my greatest admiration for him is for his humility. He had the wisdom to say that humans "don't know one-millionth of one percent about anything." How different that is from the hubris know-it-all generation in which we live. We may think that we are wise, but if we do, we are fools in the eyes of God. The wise know that to be true.

SOUL SEARCH: What am I afraid of when it comes to speaking with the unsaved? Do I fear failure, saying the wrong thing, or not being able to answer a question? What can I do to overcome this?

Father, I trust you to give me the wisdom and the words, as I step out in faith and obey your command to "preach the gospel to every creature" (Mark 16:15). Amen.

FEARFUL YOUNG MEN

The horse is prepared for the day of battle,
but deliverance is of the LORD.

—PROVERBS 21:31

I was once friends with an elderly Presbyterian minister who told me about the fear that gripped young men as they were about to enter battle in World War I. He was their chaplain, and when they came to him in tears, gripped with terror, he would read them Psalm 91.

They would do all they could to prepare themselves for battle, but each one knew his life was ultimately in the hands of God. This is a truth that many in this generation need to hear.

You and I may do all we can to try to preserve our precious lives, but if God says that our life is over, it's over. He is the only one who can keep us safe, and He's the only one who can save us from death and ultimately from hell.

SOUL SEARCH: Am I afraid of dying, or do I look forward to eternity with Jesus?

⌒

**Father, let my trust in you be the antidote of any fear
when I pass from this life. Amen.**

ADMIRING THE RICH

A good name is to be chosen rather than great riches,
loving favor rather than silver and gold.

—PROVERBS 22:1

*H*ave you noticed that not many people name their child Adolf, Judas, or Jezebel? This is because these were people whose names stunk (for want of a better word), and who would want to bear such a name?

While the world tends to admire the rich and famous, God takes note of those who have a "broken spirit … and a contrite heart" (Psalm 51:17). He notices those who trust Him. They have His smile in Christ. It is heaven we should want to please, and we can do so in Christ by being humble (James 4:6) and by "speaking the truth in love" (Ephesians 4:15). We can have a good name by loving righteousness and hating iniquity (Psalm 45:7).

However, there is something more important than having a good name. It's our name's location. Is it in the Lamb's Book of Life? That will have eternal consequences.

SOUL SEARCH: Am I involved in anything that could bring shame to the gospel? If so, what is it, and what do I need to do so that is no longer true?

**Father, never let me do anything that
would bring shame to my faith. Amen.**

EASE AND COMFORT

The rich and poor have this is common,
the Lᴏʀᴅ is the maker of them all.
—PROVERBS 22:2

*T*he rich and the poor live on different planets. The rich live a life of ease and comfort. They have no pressing mortgage to meet, no outstanding bills to pay, and no worries about not having enough food to put on the table. They have no concerns about healthcare, the education of their kids, or the gangs that infest the only areas in which they can afford to live. The poor, on the other hand, are trapped.

But there is a level playing field. The Lord made the rich and the poor, and both have to face Him on judgment day. The twist is that the poor pray. They have to because of their poverty. They are rich in faith because they are poor in this world's goods.

The rich don't need God because money supplies all their needs. Money is their god, and so they are desperately poor in what will matter in eternity.

If you're not sure where you will spend eternity, make sure.

SOUL SEARCH: Is there anything that I am cultivating—any sport, vocation, relationship, or material possession—that could potentially replace my first love of God? If so, what is it?

**Father, let me see anything as being a vile
affection if it seeks to steal my first love. Amen.**

December 27

CLEFT FOR ME

A prudent man foresees evil and hides himself,
but the simple pass on and are punished.

—PROVERBS 22:3

"Rock of Ages, cleft for me. Let me hide myself in Thee." So wrote hymn-writer Augustus Toplady, who understood the danger in which he stood. We hide from the coming wrath in Jesus. He is our shelter from the ultimate storm.

The prudent foresee evil, but the fool remains willfully blind, and how blind this evil world is! It strains out a gnat and swallows the camel (Matthew 23:24). It is concerned only with the temporal—what to eat, what to wear, and how to keep healthy and fit. It makes provision for this life only and ignores eternity.

The world thinks it has nothing to hide—and no need to hide. Yet the day will come when every one of them will pass on, and if they are in their sins, they will be punished. Our hearts should break at such a thought.

SOUL SEARCH: Do I keep judgment day and the cross ever before me? How often do I pray for the unsaved?

⁓

**Father, never let me forget what you saved me from,
and may I ever do what you saved me for. Amen.**

RICHES NOT OF THIS WORLD

By humility and the fear of the LORD
are riches and honor and life.
—PROVERBS 22:4

There are temporal riches that come from this world, and there's an honor that comes from other human beings. This life also offers a short life that ends in death. And then there are riches that are not of this world—incorruptible wealth that is stored up in heaven. There's also an honor that comes from God alone, and a life that is everlasting. The latter are the things for which we strive. We look for a kingdom that cannot be moved, and one that is everlasting.

Humility is a true self-assessment, and the humble know that anything they have comes from the hand of God. Because they know God holds their life in the palm of His hand, they fear Him. The virtues of humility and the fear of God are exemplified in the Son of God, who was "gentle and lowly in heart" (Matthew 11:29) and was "heard because of His godly fear" (Hebrews 5:7).

SOUL SEARCH: When was the last time I considered everything I have? Where do I believe it comes from?

*Father, may I walk in the fear of the Lord,
so that my prayers for the lost are heard. Amen.*

THORNS AND SNARES

Thorns and snares are in the way of the perverse;
he who guards his soul will be far from them.

—PROVERBS 22:5

The Scriptures tell us that we live in the midst of a demonic realm (Ephesians 6:12–20). Unlike the secular world, when we say, "He has his demons," we often mean it. This is because the Bible from the beginning to the end tells us that this world is filled with spiritual forces, principalities, and powers, and that the leader of it (the god of this world) came to kill, steal, and destroy. Ignore the salvation of your soul, serve the devil, and he will kill you, steal your soul, and destroy you eternally. If you serve sin, you serve the devil. Serve sin and you automatically set before yourself thorns and snares that will in finality bring you to a place of unending anguish.

But if you yield your soul to God through the Savior, you will not only save yourself pain in this life, but you will also be preserved by the grace of God in the next.

SOUL SEARCH: When was the last time I allowed the devil some leeway in my life?

**Father, today I give place to you
in every area of my life. Amen.**

TRAIN UP A CHILD

> Train up a child in the way he should go,
> and when he is old he will not depart from it.
> —PROVERBS 22:6

This verse doesn't say, "Get a decision for Jesus from your child when he's three years old, and he won't depart from it." If you do that, you may keep him in your church until girls look more attractive than Noah's ark, but then suddenly he's off into the world.

Rather, do what the Bible says. Instruct him out of the moral law. In speaking of the Ten Commandments, the Scriptures say when to do that—when you sit with him, when you walk with him, and when you lie down with him. Put the commandments on his hands and in front of his eyes (Deuteronomy 6:6–7). In doing so, the law will act as a schoolmaster to bring him to Christ (Galatians 3:24 AKJV). Train him up that way, and he will not depart from it.

SOUL SEARCH: What steps have I taken to diligently teach the younger generation your law?

⌇

**Father, please give me wisdom when speaking
to children about you. Amen.**

December 31

PAID IN FULL

The rich rules over the poor,
and the borrower is servant to the lender.

—PROVERBS 22:7

The Bible tells us that God's law is perfect (Psalm 29:7) and that we were deeply in debt to it. The only payment that would satisfy its spiritual precepts was our death and damnation; we were hopeless and helpless criminals in the face of its wrath. But Jesus became a curse for us, to redeem us from eternal death. We broke the law, but Jesus paid our fine when He died on the cross.

Our debt has been paid in full, but Jesus didn't lend us the payment. He gave it in His precious blood, such was His love for us. So we are now unprofitable servants, who, because we are forgiven so great a debt, delight to do His will. We love Him because He first loved us.

SOUL SEARCH: How does my life prove my gratefulness for God's love and Christ's death on the cross?

Father, may my life this day be an expression
of my love for you, and gratitude for the cross. Amen.

About the Author

RAY COMFORT is the best-selling author of more than eighty books. He is the co-host of an award-winning TV program that airs in 190 countries, and the producer of award-winning movies that have been seen by millions (see FullyFreeFilms.com). He lives in Southern California with his wife, Sue, and has three grown children. Connect with Ray and his many resources at LivingWaters.com.

LivingWaters.com